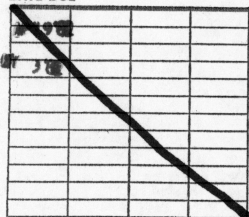

the story of Ballet

the story of **Ballet**

Joan Lawson

Taplinger Publishing Company
New York

This book is dedicated to
my friends in The Royal Ballet
and
to all 'White Lodgers'
everywhere.

Acknowledgements

This book has been written with the help of the children at
the Royal Ballet School, White Lodge, whose questions
sparked off many ideas of how I could help them understand
what makes a ballet. Not all of them will become dancers,
but I hope they will always remember what we talked about
and will remain lovers of this art, for without an audience to
understand what the dancers are trying to convey, Ballet
cannot live.

I must also thank the Director of the Royal Ballet School
and the Press Office at the Royal Opera House for allowing
me to use so many photographs from the archives held at
White Lodge, without such records my task would have
been hard. Although some of the photographers no longer
practise their art, nevertheless I must put their names on
record and ask Gordon Anthony; Arthur Carter; Deben-
ham; Dominic; Erik Dzeni; Nic Espinosa; John Hart;
Andreus Heumann; Mandinian; Derrick de Marney;
George Milford-Cottam; Photo Reproductions; Press Asso-
ciation; Houston Rogers; Roy Round; Turner Sedgwick;
M. Sorokina; Leslie E. Spatt; Michael Stannard; the Victoria
and Albert Museum; Jenny Walton; Paul Wilson; Reg
Wilson and Roger Wood to accept my very grateful thanks.
In particular I must thank my friend Anthony Crickmay,
whose work covers most of the ballet companies in the
world. Without his marvellous eye for a 'dancing picture'
and his sympathy with my ideas, my search would have
been almost impossible.

Contents

Chapter 1

Introduction

'You must dance from the tips of your toes to the tips of your fingers and upwards through your body to your head'. So said Anna Pavlova, one of the greatest dancers of the 20th century, whose exquisite dancing inspired so many people. But did they all realise how much work had gone to the making of this frail looking star? How much of her life did she give up to become that swift Dragonfly, the delicate Californian Poppy, a wind-swept Autumn Leaf, or that tragic Dying Swan? Her dances depicting some of the beauties of Nature live forever in the memories of those who saw her performances. But did they all realise that not only did she possess natural gifts, like her delicate physique and her intense musical understanding, but also that she had perfected the many aspects of her great art through her unwearying studies in the school-room.

The dancer and dancing are not the only things in Ballet. Ballet needs the co-operation of many arts. It can tell a story like *The Sleeping Beauty* or *Giselle*, describe a scene like skaters in *Les Patineurs*, as well as being pure dancing as in *Symphonic Variations*. In all ballets there must be music to phrase the dance and suggest the emotions, actions and moods of the dancers. There must be scenery and costume to give time and place to the story. There must be choreography, that is dance movement which will help the dancers to tell that story, express their moods and emotions and make clear their characters. Dancers have to tell that story without words, speaking instead with the whole body and it is the work of the choreographer to design the dance or mime scenes and to arrange these movements on the stage so that the audience understands what the dancers are saying.

But this is not all. The dancers first of all have to be taught to dance in such a way that every step and pose is seen to its best advantage from the audience's point of view. The present-day stage is a room, only one side of which is open to the audience, so choreographers and dancers must always remember to direct themselves towards the audience not only as they dance, but also as they act out their parts, perhaps using one of the three forms of mime. Then they must learn to use make-up, for their features would look pale and blurred under the stage lights if they did not paint their faces and enlarge their eyes. The eyes are the most important features of a dancer's face. They lead the movement, they direct attention to the other dancers. They express emotion and mood. As John Weaver, the first of the great English teachers of dance said, 'They are the mirror of the soul'.

Perhaps you would like to dance like Anna Pavlova, Vaslav Nijinsky, Tamara Karsavina, Margot Fonteyn and the present stars of The Royal Ballet, or those others at

Above: mime in Stuttgart

Right: Anna Pavlova

the Kirov and Bolshoi theatres in the U.S.S.R., in famous companies all over the world from Australia to France, Canada to Italy. Perhaps you too feel you could fly like 'The Firebird' as she comes to the help of the Tsarevich, or triumphantly rule your kingdom like Princess Aurora after her Prince has awakened her with a kiss in *The Sleeping Beauty*, or even play cat's cradle and make butter like Lise, the farmer's daughter in *La Fille Mal Gardée*. Before you do so you will have to spend at least seven years sometimes longer – studying the rules and vocabulary of dance and gesture in the classrooms, and at the same time learning about music, art, literature, history and other languages and even mathematics, for many patterns and steps have to be exact in measurement and placing, as the lines made as the dancer moves over the stage must make pictures pleasing to the eyes of the audience.

The Dancer's Physique

Classical dance makes heavy demands on all the muscles of your body, particularly on your spine and pelvis because you turn your legs outwards within the hip-joints. This means that all the muscles of your legs and upwards through your spine have to be stretched, strengthened and then used in a slightly different way than in ordinary movement. If you have always enjoyed your dancing lessons and have decided by the time you are ten years old and that you would like to become a dancer, you must apply for an audition at one of the professional dancing schools where they also teach general subjects. Before you go, take a good

Dancer's physique, the boy in Leningrad

Dancer's physique, the girl

look at yourself in a long mirror and see if your body, legs, arms and head look like a dancer's. The teachers who watch you performing simple exercises and improvising a little dance will be carefully studying six important things about you.

1. Is your body well proportioned? This means your legs and arms not being either too long or too short in proportion to your body.
2. Are your legs quite straight as they face the front? The middle toe of your foot should be directly in front of the middle of your ankle and under the middle of your knee and thigh.
3. Is your head a pleasing shape or is it too large or too small? Can you move it freely from side to side and up and down? Does your neck rise centrally between your two shoulders and is your head held erect? Are your shoulders, like your hips, quite level? A dancer has to balance on both or one leg in many different positions, so both sides of the body should be equal in size and length. Very often when you are growing one leg or arm can be a little longer than the other, but it generally evens out eventually.
4. Do your legs and arms move easily in their sockets? Try and swing first one and then the other leg, or one arm and then the other forwards and backwards without moving any other part of your body. You will have to tilt your body

forwards from the hinge-like joint at the top of your leg if you first lift it to the back. Otherwise you should not have to move your body at all. Can you circle your leg by stretching it forward as far as possible, fully pointed toe on the floor, and then move it round to the back and bring it forward again without twisting your hips? Use first one and then the other leg like the pencil in a pair of compasses to draw a semi-circle at the side of the supporting leg.

5. When you dance do you listen to the music and as Fokine, one of the greatest choregraphers, said: 'Dance to, through and from the music?' That is what you have to do when you dance in his beautiful ballet, *Les Sylphides*.

6. Do the parts of your body co-ordinate and flow when you start to dance so that you do as Pavlova said at the beginning of this book?

If you can answer 'yes' to all these questions and if those watching you agree, and offer you a place in the school, and if you really believe you want to be a dancer enough to be prepared to learn all the rules and all the subjects that go to make a dancer and a ballet, then you will be given a thorough medical examination where your eyes, ears, heart, lungs, nose – in fact every part of your body – will be tested. You may have some simple defect with which you were born like knock-knees, or sway-back legs, which if slight, can be corrected by proper training. It is not so easy to train, loosen or strengthen some types of spine. Nor can too short hamstrings or tight achilles tendons be stretched, although such problems can be lessened if they are only fairly minor ones. In the 236-year-old school in Leningrad in the U.S.S.R. the medical examination usually takes place first of all because the teachers there prefer not to disappoint anybody they might have selected if the doctors say 'No', perhaps because of a weak heart or poor lungs. The discipline of the eight year course in the twenty-five ballet schools of the U.S.S.R. is so strict and energetic that only very healthy children can be accepted. This does not mean they look tough. A glance at the fairy-like Anna Pavlova or the English ballerina Antoinette Sibley, tells you that strength is not always shown outwardly. It is the inward determination that makes the dancer.

Life at School

Once you are accepted at any professional school you must be ready and willing for hard work. Whether you are a boarder or go daily your syllabus is more or less the same all over the world. Classical dancing lessons take their place in the time-table along with general lessons for five if not six days a week. During your first year at school dancing lessons usually last about 1¼ hours a day. By the time you are fifteen or sixteen the time has increased to 1½ to 2 hours. After this, when you have taken your General Certificate or other school leaving certificate, your classical dancing lesson lasts 2 hours and you have many other dance studies throughout the day.

But the daily classical dance class is not the only dance activity during a week. At the Royal Ballet Junior School,

White Lodge, there will be one or two coaching classes for all the boys and girls. The boys also start studying our traditional Sword and Morris dances in their first years and graduate to Clog dancing in their third year. (This ensures that there will always be someone to play Mother Simone in *La Fille Mal Gardée*, where her clog dance is so important!) They also join the girls in English country dancing which teaches them how to behave towards their partners and teaches the girls how to accept their help. The same thing happens in the Soviet schools, where the children study their traditional folk dances from their first year. Later on boys and girls study character dance and, in their fifth year, the more difficult art of *pas de deux*, where the girl has to balance perhaps on the toes of one foot whilst the boy circles round her holding her hand firmly or lifts her from the floor in a jump.

A typical day at White Lodge begins with the rising bell. The pupils must wash, dress and be ready for breakfast at 8 a.m. Afterwards they return to their dormitories, make their beds, tidy up, collect all they need for dancing and school work and have to be ready in their class or dressing-room in time to get to the studio by 8.45 a.m. to start work. The day children arrive by school bus in time for the three older forms to have their dancing lessons between 8.45 a.m. and 1.15 p.m. There are six morning dance sessions in the two big studios as boys and girls always work separately, while the general education syllabus is divided into five sessions each morning with a break for drink and biscuits.

The first pair of ballet shoes in Moscow

Social Dance class for the First Form in Leningrad

Above and below: Court Dances for senior students in Leningrad

White Lodge boys in a sword dance

White Lodge boys' 'Morris Capers'

The afternoon dance time-table is divided so that Forms 1 and 2 each have a longer lesson, boys and girls again being taught separately. The general lessons are divided into three sessions. Thus in any one day each pupil has one dancing and at least five ordinary lessons before tea.

Afterwards there may be extra dancing for some, homework and the important washing of tights and darning, cleaning and preparing shoes. Both boys and girls are taught to manage all these vital things for themselves. Day children stay for any extra dancing, but take homework away to do on their journey or at home where they too have to wash and prepare their wardrobe. Clean shoes, socks, tights, tunics, shirts and underclothes are essential at all times.

The whole of Saturday morning is devoted to some kind of dancing and in the afternoon some children go home for the rest of the week-end, or parents may come to take them out. Others may be lucky and go to a matinée at the Opera House. Only twelve seats are available to the Junior School for each matinée so this privilege is shared as fairly as possible. Sunday is a rest day perhaps going to church, walking in the park, visiting some interesting place or going to see a friend, playing games, reading or watching television.

In addition most children study some musical instrument as they do in all Soviet Choregraphic Schools, so time has to be found for lessons and practice. Special music rooms have been built and pianos seem to be everywhere and well used.

White Lodge pupils rehearse *The Nutcracker* with Rudolph Nureyev, Antoinette Sibley and Anthony Dowell at the Opera House

At the age of 15–16 those fifth form pupils of the Royal Ballet Junior School who have proved their ability to dance, graduate to the Upper School in Baron's Court where they join in classes with students from other schools and countries. Not all of them stop their general education. Some of the most gifted frequently continue to study for their A. Level English Literature, History, French, Art and Music. But they are few because the students' time-table is full. There is the daily classical class, the weekly lessons in mime, character and Spanish dance, double work, make-up, studying how to write down dances – even whole ballets – in Benesh Notation and then performing what has been written down under the exacting eyes of a ballet-master or teacher. There are the weekly lectures on such things as The History of Ballet, Drama, Art, Musical Appreciation. Each of the fourteen classes also has lessons on the repertoire and virtuosity. This means studying most of the *corps de ballet* and solo dances in the important ballets of the company's repertoire so that at any time a boy or girl from the topmost classes can be called in if there is a 'flu epidemic or some other problem to take somebody's place in a ballet such as *Giselle* or *Swan-Lake*. These classes also prepare the students for the parts they will dance in the Annual Students' Matinée at the Royal Opera House, when the entire cast is made up of students.

Performances

The annual school matinée is not however the only· opportunity the Royal Ballet students have of appearing on the stage. As in all the famous ballet companies of the world, children are, from their first days at school, given chances to appear. Perhaps they are only pages carrying King Florestan's cloak in *The Sleeping Beauty*, or children dancing simple steps at the party in *The Nutcracker* or performing the more complicated dances as soldiers and rats in the same ballet. One may even appear as a soloist when someone is needed to play the Changeling Boy in Sir Frederick Ashton's *The Dream*.

All such performances give children studying at professional schools everywhere the experience they need and an understanding of the strict discipline required behind scenes before they tackle their Annual Performances, which usually take place at the end of the school year. These .require weeks of careful planning of rehearsals and cast changes, particularly in England where the annual performances coincide with the yearly examinations that are so important for those about to leave the Junior School at the age of 15–16. In the U.S.S.R. there is no division between the Junior and Senior Schools. There the general certificate examination is taken at 14–15 so that the last three years at school only involve special examinations such as The History of Ballet and the final Graduation Examination in Dance. This is a most exciting event. The students appear in a general class taken by their own teacher, then each one dances firstly as a member of a *corps de ballet* made up of his

Antoinette Sibley makes her début as Swanhilda at the Students' Matinée

or her own class-mates and secondly as a soloist or partner in whichever type of dance his or her teacher feels is the most suitable. The dance can be purely classical like a solo from *The Sleeping Beauty*; romantic like a *pas de deux* or solo from *Giselle*; demicharacter like a solo from *La Fille Mal Gardée*; or character like the Russian, Hungarian or Spanish dances from *Swan Lake* or *The Nutcracker*. The Graduation Examinations are usually directed by the foremost dancer of his or her day. In Moscow this is often their beloved star, People's Artiste Galina Ulanova, with some other stars from the Bolshoi, a leading conductor, directors of other dance and ballet companies and always the Director of the Moscow Choregraphic Academy, People's Artiste Sophie Golovkina and her staff. In England both pupils and students take the appropriate examinations of The Royal Academy of Dancing, the Cecchetti Society or the British Ballet Organisation at intervals during their seven or eight years at school. Their final test and perhaps entry into one of the Royal Ballet Companies is often determined by the way they dance at the annual matinée.

Progress at School

Of course not everyone entering a professional school at the age of 10–11 stays for the whole course. When you enter as a new pupil you are given a trial year and it is up to you to prove that you want to and can be a dancer. But many things can happen. Sometimes you, the pupil, realise that the discipline required to train your body and mind is too strict and you feel it does not let you 'just dance', like you did in your first dancing lessons. The daily exercises performed first at the barre, repeated in the centre and then across or round the room can seem monotonous for they have to be performed every day. This does not mean that they are always exactly the same. Far from it, because the best teachers change each exercise even during the first lessons. It may only be to make you bend and stretch your legs in the first *pliés* to a slow march or mazurka instead of a waltz. Perhaps to raise your arm above your head as your knees bend instead of dropping it in front of your legs. There are so many ways and timings of each exercise and these slight changes help you to understand that if, much later, you join a company, you will not find it difficult to break the rules set by your first teacher. The choreographer often breaks the rules. For example you are taught in classical dances that the arms should always be curved except in *arabesque* when they straighten. But Sir Frederick Ashton often gives his dancers' arms very straight lines in his beautiful *Symphonic Variations*. But even with these changes in the exercises some pupils feel bored and frustrated, and it will show in their dancing.

Sometimes the shape of your body changes as you grow. This is quite natural and nobody so far has been able to predict exactly *how* you will grow. There is a way of telling approximately how tall you will be and this method is used for everybody coming into the Royal Ballet Junior School.

Boys' and girls' *ports de bras* with Betty Oliphant at the national Ballet School in Toronto

Getting into a Company

Earlier it was noted how a student's performance at the Annual School matinée can decide if he or she will be taken into the Company for which the school trains dancers. As the director, choreographer, ballet-masters and teachers of that company already know the students through constant watching of classes and rehearsals, the ones who are likely to be invited to join the Company have already been picked out long before the matinée. Nevertheless the good news is usually held up until after the curtain comes down, when the names are announced before an excited but apprehensive cast.

If you are unlucky and have not been chosen, there are other avenues open; indeed you may have been warned quite early in your last school year that you are unlikely to be among the lucky ones. As soon as you know definitely, and if you are still determined to dance, you should look elsewhere for work. Nowadays there are many companies throughout the world who need well-trained dancers to perform in the ballets presented in the opera houses and State theatres of Europe, Australasia, America and elsewhere. Ballet-masters in such theatres require dancers who do not think it beneath their dignity to dance in operas and operettas containing ballets, to appear as pages, or even merely to swell the crowd scenes. This is marvellous experience because it gives you such a range of music and production to study. You can dance as a peasant or bacchante in Gounod's *Faust*, as a Negro or Egyptian slave in *Aida*, or a street dancer in *Carmen* or *Porgy and Bess*. Most of these companies also stage evenings of ballet when you and your colleagues have the theatre to yourselves. Your repertoire may contain such varied works as Fokine's *Les Sylphides* to music by Chopin, the Fokine-Stravinsky *The Firebird*, or *Petrushka* and your own ballet-master's works to some modern composer like Hans Werner Henze or Berio.

Some towns in the British Isles – including Cork, Glasgow and Manchester – and throughout Europe and the U.S.A. have their own smaller ballet companies. Wherever you are, you should write to these asking for an audition. Sometimes, particularly if you are writing abroad, it is a good idea to write to several towns in the same country or area and if you get replies asking you to come for an audition, make a short tour. Wherever you go, you will usually be expected to join in a company class and dance one or two excerpts or solos of your own choice. You may also be asked if you know anything of modern dance. Most ballet-masters insist on every member of the company having a sound classical dance training because they know such dancers can always manage many different styles, their bodies having been properly prepared. But they also know that audiences of today like to see experimental ballets from time to time. When you dance in these strange movements, sounds and ideas can tax your body, ears and brain. Have you the courage to face such works?

Company Class at the Bolshoi

It is no good accepting a girl who will grow very tall because there will be no partner tall enough to lift her. When a girl is *sur les pointes*, it is very difficult for her male partner to work with her if she is taller than he is. Similarly if a boy is going to be too short, it is unlikely he will be accepted for training unless he happens to have very unusual talents.

Sometimes the teachers decide that you have not fulfilled the promise you showed at the audition. Perhaps you have not bothered to work hard enough. Perhaps the slight difficulty you had with your turn-out, tight achilles tendon, hamstrings or stiff back is not responding to their teaching no matter how hard and carefully they try. They have to be very careful because many perfectly natural changes are taking place while you are growing and you must not be allowed to strain in any way to achieve that turn-out, to stretch and straighten your spine and develop your correct stance.

If at the end of your first year there is still some doubt about your talent, you will probably be given a second year's trial but will have to leave after this if you are obviously going to grow too tall or if other faults still worry those who are assessing your progress. This possibility of having to leave at the end of any year continues throughout the five years of the junior section of every professional school I have ever visited. But after this it is rare for any student to be asked to go except in exceptional circumstances where serious illness, accident or sometimes personal circumstances, makes dancing impossible as a career.

Top right: Northern Dance Theatre in Laverne Meyer's *Cinderella*

Right: Scottish Ballet in Peter Darrell's *Tales of Hoffmann*

Working in a Company

Once you are accepted into a company – and it does not matter where – the routine is always the same, although the time-table will change from day to day to fit in with each particular performance and theatre. The daily class of 1–1½ hours is always taken first thing in the morning, whether you have a performance that night or not. This class may be followed by rehearsals, wardrobe and shoe-fitting or special coaching if you have to learn the repertoire. If you are in a small touring company like *Ballet For All*, you may have to travel to the next town early in the morning and be given the so-called 'Company Class' just before an afternoon performance. This class is always given no more than 1½ hours before any performance of ballet anywhere. It is essential that no dancer appears before an audience 'cold'. Even children appearing as pages are given a 'warm-up' before walking on so that, like their seniors, their whole bodies are tuned up and ready to work easily and correctly when the ballet begins.

On tour these classes and rehearsals can take place in most dismal, dirty halls, large, draughty rooms and odd corners of theatres. Very few theatres have the magnificent facilities of the Theatre of Opera and Ballet named Kirov in Leningrad (the old Maryinsky). When its stage was re-built after war-time bombing, the Leningrad Soviet erected a huge new building by its side. This not only contains an exact replica of the stage, orchestra pit, lighting and other important equipment, with seats for an audience of 120, but also music and concert halls, dressing rooms and five enormous studios for the singers, musicians and dancers. In the studios dancers have their daily classes and rehearsals and study new roles under the guidance of the chief ballet-master, choreographer and teachers.

Above: Wayne Sleep takes a class

Below: Alexander Pushkin takes a class in Leningrad

Dégas: *Fin d'Arabesque*

Tamara Karsavina as Columbine in *Carnaval*

If you join a touring company you often have problems finding 'digs' in which to rest your tired bones after a day's work or a long journey. Digs have become increasingly scarce as more and more theatres have closed down for want of audiences. However they can usually be found with perseverance. But there have been times when the dancers have just had to sleep in the theatre, or on the train if the company is making a tour of 'One Night Stands'. In these cases it is more usual, if the company is large to hire a whole train which became 'home' as the Royal Ballet did during a six-week tour in the U.S.A. In some cases a small company owns a motor coach, which becomes its home, the group travelling, eating and sleeping on the road before appearing in church, school or village halls or cheerfully making the best of it in some old theatre or even warehouse.

All such activities can be tremendous fun and very rewarding when you feel you have really brought pleasure to your audience. But such audiences are not always ready to applaud. It is up to you to give out all you know generously and with feeling. Help them to understand how much you want them to enjoy the work you love and how the inconvenience and difficulties you have had to put up with are nothing compared to your enjoyment in dance. They have often come to see you in order to take their minds off their own worries and nothing in your bearing should give any inkling that there is no heat in the dressing-room, that the stage-roof leaks, that your new shoes have not arrived from the makers, and that you feel awful. You must forget the hundred and one vexations that can take your mind off your dancing unless you concentrate and lose yourself in your particular part.

You may of course be lucky enough to go into a resident company which merely visits nearby towns and in this case you can share a flat with friends. This is an excellent arrangement, but also brings other responsibilities such as payments for rent, light, heating and so on. When you are working abroad there will be various extra taxes. You will also be expected to help keep the flat clean, shop and cook your own meals and perform other domestic jobs. This is the time when the French, German or other language you learnt so reluctantly at school can be of great value.

You may think I have spent too much time on the problems of daily life and not enough on dancing. But you have a duty to your company and your audience to keep yourself healthy all the time. You must therefore ask yourself honestly if you really are capable of coping with life outside as well as inside the ballet theatre and classroom. Can you bear to refuse all those invitations to parties and exciting trips? Have you the strength of mind to leave early because you must have some proper sleep before the nine o'clock company class, followed by make-up and a full dress rehearsal with orchestra from 10.30 a.m. until 2 p.m.; a rush up to the wardrobe to have your dress made more comfortable, a brief rest before the company class at 5.30 p.m. and the curtain call for Les Sylphides at 7.30, when you must be silent and calm, ready to answer the call of the music as if in a dream? Such days are fairly common in the world of ballet and a day where there is only the morning class is welcome, because you can now really wash all those tights and underclothes, and darn all those new ballet shoes before you set out for the next day's work.

Very few dancers graduate from school straight into the ranks of soloist like Anna Pavlova, Vaslav Nijinsky, Tamara Karsavina and Mikhail Fokine. Most go straight into the corps de ballet and rise to stardom through sheer hard work and willingness to cope with any task put to them. Some are immediately kept busy dancing in every ballet, thus proving they have the stamina and brain to learn their particular place in the patterns of the dances quickly and without hindering the older dancers. Others are not kept so busy, perhaps because their height does not match that of the dancers already being used, perhaps because they learn slowly. But both types of entrant to the company should lose no opportunity of watching every possible rehearsal and performance so as to be able to step into any place at a moment's notice. It often happens, even on the stage itself, that someone is taken ill and a new member of the company, who has taken the trouble to study the part for herself or himself, comes on and dances it successfully. This kind of keenness cannot fail to make a very favourable impression and such a dancer has often risen quickly through the ranks to become a star.

But stars are not the main reason for the success of any ballet. Everyone who is involved, either on or off stage has a part to play. The great director Serge Diaghilev, whose Russian Ballet when it first danced in Paris in 1909 changed the whole structure and future of our art, insisted that all were equal. Even though his leading dancers were great stars in their own right, their dancing would not have made the impression it did without the perfect co-operation and co-ordination of all the other dancers, artists, musicians and stage staff making the ballet. Strangely enough the ballet that made the greatest impression of all was not the delicate Les Sylphides but the barbaric, primitive Polovtsian Dances from Prince Igor. Never before had such wildly exciting leaps, turns and unbounded energy been seen on any European stage. But the dancers' enthusiasm and belief in this ballet created by Fokine, Borodin, the composer and Roerich, the artist was such that they overwhelmed their audience by generously giving themselves to their task and to those who watched.

The Rules of Classical Dance

The Polovtsian Dances from Prince Igor were so different from Coppélia and other 19th century ballets that the audience found it difficult to believe these Russian dancers had ever been taught in the same classical way as those at the Paris Opera. But they had, and so will you be if you go to a professional school. As you learn to dance you also begin to learn something of the history of our art and how it became what it now is.

The first teachers of dance were the Troubadours in the Provençal courts, at the time of the Crusades. It was then that the simple steps of country folk became neater as the courtiers glided over smoother floors instead of dancing on cobbles and village greens. One of these noble minstrels wrote a dance-song, 'Advice to a Young Lady' telling her how to behave when dancing with her knight. Amongst the advice given is how to hold yourself, your dress and head with its high head-dress and how to bow to your partner's compliments and take his hand. You still have to hold your body correctly and move your arms with grace and your head with dignity.

Later, in 1581, Canon Arbeau of Langres in France wrote out his advice to Capriol, a young friend about to dance at court. Arbeau gives his rules for behaviour in general and to the partner in particular. He speaks of the four positions of the feet, which are like our 1st, 2nd, 3rd and 4th positions. These help to balance the body gracefully because Arbeau insists that a slight turn-out of the legs will make the steps easier and more elegant as they show off the well-pointed foot. But what Arbeau feels is most important is to make Capriol understand how his steps must fit the music. This is something that is vitally important whenever you dance.

At the end of the 17th century King Louis XIV of France founded the Académie de Danse within the Académie Royale de Musique (1672) and Beauchamp, his dancing-master, began to work out exactly how each step was to be performed. He first described the five positions of the feet as we use them today which are essential because in every one of them both feet are firmly placed on the floor to enable you to recover your balance between one step or pose and an-

Beauchamp, dancing-master to Louis XIV

other. He also described exactly how to dance such simple steps as a *chassé*, *glissade*, and *pas de bourrée* with turned-out feet, as we do today.

It was in 1706 that an English dancing-master, John Weaver, dancing-master of Shrewsbury Grammar School, who also danced and taught in London, translated a book by Feuillet, Beauchamp's pupil. He was the first man to help dancers understand the connection between the bones, ligaments, tendons and muscles and the dance movements. To do this he described the four ways of moving the various parts of the body by using the muscles. The movements are: 1. To bend; 2. To stretch; 3. To rise, raise or spring; and 4. To turn or circle. He writes about one of the most important rules of balance – 'The Natural Law of Opposition', in which the arm that is raised forward is always to the foot that is in front, whether that foot is supporting you or lifted from the floor. But you must never allow your leg or arm to cross the centre of your body if you want to balance calmly. This is something very important to remember during your dancing lessons.

Weaver wrote several books on dance and its history and always stressed the importance of the use of the head and eyes, just as your teacher will do today, for example when teaching you how to 'spot' in a *pirouette*.

In 1760 Jean-Georges Noverre, a great French dancing-master wrote his *Letters on the Dance*. He followed John Weaver's rules but added many more. By this time ballet was no longer danced by elegant courtiers, but by professionals who did not use such simple steps. Noverre described the seven movements of dance which we use today in class and which are still called by their French names. They are :–

1. *Plier* – to bend. (Noun: *plié*).
2. *Tendir* or *étendre* – to stretch. (Adjective: *tendu*).
3. *Relever* or *élever* – to rise or raise. (Noun or adjective: *relevé* or *élevé*).
4. *Sauter* – to jump. (Noun: *saut* or *jeté*; adjectives: *sauté* or *jeté*).
5. *Glisser* – to glide. (Noun: *glissade* or *chassé*; adjectives: *glissé* or *chassé*).
6. *Élancer* – to dart. (Adjective: *élancé*).
7. *Tourner* – to turn. (Noun: *Tour* or *pirouette*).

An important rule which also helps you to place your body and always face correctly in the proper direction was Noverre's 'Law of Natural *Épaulement*'. This is: as you spring from foot to foot in steps like *petits jetés* bring the same shoulder forwards as foot in front. There are many more rules written by Noverre which you will use as you dance. Although he was not the first teacher to demand that costumes should be made lighter than the ladies' long heavy skirts and the equally heavy tonnelets worn by the gentleman, to give the legs more room and make dancing easier, he was the first to put his demands into print.

It was in 1820 that the great Italian dancing-master, Carlo Blasis wrote his first book, which he later enlarged to become *The Code of Terpsichore*, named in honour of the Greek goddess of Dance. (She is one of the Muses who teach the young Apollo in Balanchine's ballet *Apollo*.) In the book

Children of the Bryan Lawrence School in Canberra, Australia,
demonstrate *to bend, to stretch and raise, to rise, to jump*

An *attitude* in Leningrad

1. Natural balance and dignity.
2. Natural ease and an ability to move gracefully.
3. Ability to work out how steps and poses melt into a dance.
4. Knowledge and use of all the rules at all times.
5. Realisation of what the dancer can do and what suits him or her best when dancing in any ballet.
6. Interest in the art, and knowledge of what every ballet is about.
7. Study of music and drawing to help with the understanding of how to phrase and draw movements through the air and on the ground.

August Bournonville, the great Danish teacher, however, required much more from his dancers than Blasis. He had studied and travelled all over Europe, which gave him inspiration for many ballets when he became ballet-master of the King's Theatre, Copenhagen. Amongst those which are still performed are Scottish dances in *La Sylphide*, Spanish in *Far From Denmark* and exciting Italian ones in *Napoli*. His methods of teaching us to jump were taken to

Above: *développé devant* from Georgina Parkinson of the Royal Ballet

Right: David Wall, *grand elevation* for the Royal Ballet

you can find all the rules upon which our dancing is based. Blasis worked at La Scala, Milan, in Paris and in Moscow. But his importance spread because his ideas were taken everywhere by his pupils, amongst them Lepri, whose pupil, Maestro Cecchetti did so much to perfect the dancing of those great Russian artists Pavlova, Karsavina and Nijinsky and others, including the founders of English ballet, Dame Marie Rambert and Dame Ninette de Valois.

Amongst the many rules Blasis laid down were how to balance and how to *pirouette*. The former teaches you how to centre your weight by pulling your spine up straight so that the crown of your head is directly over the centre of one or both feet. The latter teaches you how to use your head and arm as you turn. Blasis also invented the beautiful pose known as the 'Mercury attitude' which he named after a statue by Gian Bologna and was the first to describe an *arabesque* with the leg raised high from the ground, the body and head describing the beautiful curve that is found in Moorish architecture.

But perhaps the most important thing Blasis taught was that the teacher must look for seven things when the pupil danced.

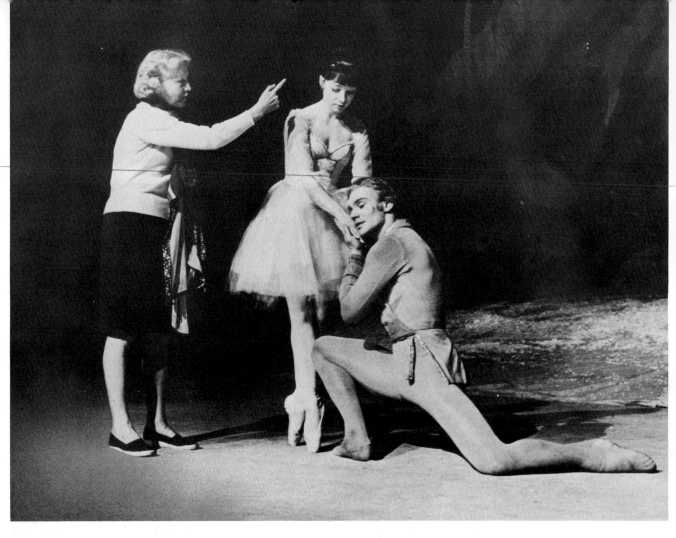

Galina Ulanova coaches Ekaterina Maximova and Yuri Vassiliev in
Cinderella for the Bolshoi Ballet

Saint Petersburg, by his pupil Johannsen who in turn taught those warriors of the *Polovtsian Dances* from *Prince Igor* and stars like Nijinsky so to leap that it looked as though they stayed still in the air. This secret has gradually been acquired by all other schools as Russian teachers spread abroad. But it may take at least five years before boy or girl can seem to 'hover' like a bird while flying through the air. Some dancers never manage this, though they may make up for it by having other valuable qualities.

Because Blasis taught how to balance more easily, women dancers rose higher on their toes until they could balance and spin *sur les pointes* and it became possible for Pierina Legnani to spin round thirty-two times on one toe in the famous 32 *pirouettes fouettés en tournant* at the first performance of *Swan-Lake*. But it takes a long time to do this – at least six months of daily lessons before you are taught gradually to rise through your feet to stand on tip-toe. And at least five years before you may manage to spin round like Legnani even twelve times. Of course you may eventually manage more, but, as with *grand elevation* (big jumps) some dancers never manage this, although their performance can please the audience.

It was because Bournonville realised that it was not enough for dancers just to learn to jump, turn and know all the rules that he demanded much more from those he chose to become his pupils. In the same way that all professional schools look for something more than just a pretty face, good physique and legs, Bournonville wanted his dancers to have :–

1. Beauty, suppleness, vivacity and concentration.
2. Good taste, energy, perseverance, imagination and co-ordination.
3. Grace, lightness, dignity, manners and precision.
4. Presence, carriage, personality, expression and gesture.
5. Well-placed, turned-out, well-pointed feet, ability to jump softly and easily and brilliant technique.

Like Bournonville and Blasis the directors, ballet-masters, choreographers and teachers of today do not only look at your figure and your face. They also want to know if you really understand about your art, the part you play and the ballet in which you dance. If you perhaps come on the stage as a Wili in *Giselle*, a ranch girl in *Rodeo*, a puppet in *Petrushka* or Harlequin in *Carnaval* have you really thought yourself into that part, and can you live it on the stage? Or are you still the same as when we meet in the street?

A study of the history of ballet will help you to transport yourself into another world, another period of time, a world of imagination. We dancers, until recently, have always learnt our rôles from each other, particularly from older dancers who have wonderful memories. Even now, when there are ways of writing down a ballet, it is still those older dancers who help us most by their example, understanding and love of the parts they played in the whole ballet.

22

Chapter 2
the History of Ballet Begins

'I have piped unto ye, but ye have not danced'. So sang some early Christian priests. They sang about the words of God and how His people had disobeyed His Commands. Today Indian dancers, like those ancient priests perform in dance the deeds of their god, the great Shiva. Their movements show how he created the world and all within it, man and woman, birds, beasts, flowers and the rest. In the Greek plays presented in honour of their gods dancers expressed their emotions, moods and actions as the actors told well-known stories about the gods of Olympus and what happened when heroes and heroines like Achilles, Oedipus, Medea, and Hecuba disobeyed the Three Fates. Later, Roman slaves and actors danced and mimed stories like those of Hercules or Daphnis and Chloe. As well as performing inside palaces they appeared in huge open-air theatres and circuses and every movement describing mood and emotion had to be made crystal clear so that it could be seen and understood by the furthest spectator. Ballet-masters used and still use such ancient stories, for it is from such beginnings that our present day ballet has grown. It has taken a long time and on the way has collected new themes and ideas, that have been changed and developed by choreographers, dancers, teachers, composers and artists from many different countries. Because dancers need no words and use only their bodies to convey meaning, ballet has become a universal art. This is why Anna Pavlova and so many other dancers since she died have been able to dance all over the world before Zulu warriors, Malayan fishermen, Kings and Queens and peoples of all nationalities. To everyone who saw her, Anna Pavlova was the Dying Swan, as Tamara Karsavina was the Firebird, Margot Fonteyn was Princess Aurora and Nijinsky was Petrushka.

It was not until the Renaissance and after Catherine de Medici married Henry II of France, that a special type of court entertainment began to be called ballet. Catherine came from Florence where learned men, like those in other Northern Italian towns staged great spectacles in honour of an important event. It might be a wedding uniting the son and daughter of two noble Princes who had been fighting each other; it might be the founding of an Order of Knighthood. This was the case when the Duke of Savoy started the Order of the Golden Fleece in 1420. The Bishop of Savoy preached a sermon telling these new knights that,

like Jason and the Argonauts setting out to find the Golden Fleece, they were setting out to rescue Jerusalem from the Turks. After the sermon some mimes danced into the great hall and acted out the story of Jason. Stories for ballets have come from old Greek and Roman myths and legends, others, like *Raymonda* have come from tales of the Crusades. Ballet stories are often about noble knights rescuing fair ladies from evil magicians, as happens in *Swan-Lake*.

The story of Jason and the Golden Fleece was also used when Bergonzi di Botta staged a magnificent dinner-ballet for the wedding of the Duke of Milan in 1489. His servants entered the banqueting hall dancing and singing that they had brought the Golden Fleece back from Colchis and laid a magnificent golden table-cloth on the table. Then followed various gods, goddesses and their attendants making their *entrées* – a term still used to mark the entrance of dancers in any ballet. Neptune, the sea-god drawn by dolphins and mermaids brought the fish; Diana the huntress and her nymphs brought venison and wild boar; Orpheus roast peacocks and swans; Bacchus and his Satyrs brought the wine; Ceres the fruit and so on. After the guests had eaten, a dance competition took place in which all those wives who had been faithful to their husbands during long absences, like Penelope, the wife of Ulysses, danced and defeated those who had been unfaithful like Helen of Troy.

The Ballets de Cour

However Catherine de Medici's reasons for staging her Ballets de Cour were more than mere entertainment. When her three sons, one after the other inherited the French throne, the struggle between the Catholics and Protestants in France grew bitter. She was determined to bring peace, and with the help of seven wise Frenchmen, calling themselves the Pleiades staged ballets at court that were designed to show the foolishness of such conflicts. These entertainments were produced by Catherine's Valet de Chambre, Belgiojoso or Beaujoyeulx as he was called in France. This Italian dancing-master and musician staged one of the most magnificent of all ballets the *Ballet Comique*

Margot Fonteyn and Christopher Gable in Ashton's *Daphnis and Chloe*

de la Reyne at the wedding between the Duc de Joyeuse and Margeurite de Lorraine in 1581. It told how Circe trapped the Argonauts in her magic garden and changed them into beasts because of their evil ways. Thus in the garden at the back of the hall were seen a serpent representing envy, a boar representing greed and a peacock representing pride among others. The wise men who wrote the words of the ballet hoped that this idea would show certain courtiers that if they did not repent their evil ways, peace would never come 'to the Fair Land of France'. But this was not the only part of the ballet to have a deeper meaning. There was also the scenery, like 'the Vault of Heaven', a large box covered with golden clouds and bespangled with stars. In

it sat a choir whose song represented the 'music of the spheres', which kept the world moving. Even patterns made by the dancers' feet were supposed to be significant just as the Farandole danced in *The Sleeping Beauty* and the *Syrtos* danced at Greek weddings represent the way from childhood to adult life.

With so much to look at and understand it is not surprising that only courtiers who had been taught that 'Truth is hidden in myth and image' could understand such ballets. In the same way some modern ballets are difficult for every member of the audience to understand, even though the movements may be interesting to watch.

At the Court of the Sun King

When Louis XIV came to the throne in 1643 his advisers were determined to make the French court the most powerful and magnificent in Europe. Their entertainments became even more spectacular, particularly when staged in the newly built Palace of Versailles. The meaning of each ballet became more complicated than it had been at the time of Catherine de Medici because ballets were now organised by the new academies who laid down rules which all artists working for the Royal court had to obey. Members of the Académie Française decided the rules of grammar, the meaning of each word, how to plan the plot and the dialogues or poems telling the story of each ballet. They also decreed the order in which the characters, played and danced by Princess of the Royal blood and the courtiers, had to appear. The highest rank always came last, just as today in the older ballets many ballerinas and their partners are the last to come on the stage. Louis XIV himself often appeared in his favourite part as Apollo, King of the Sun, King of the Muses. This meant that the final and most spectacular *entrée* was always made by the king before whom all had to bow. Other wise men from the Academy of Sculpture decided the type, shape, colour and meaning of the scenery and costumes. Those from the Academy of Music determined the order of the dances and their time and key signatures, speed and phrasing. Finally wise men working for the Academy of Inscriptions and Belles Lettres were responsible for choosing the plot and meaning behind each ballet.

The Opera-Ballets

Louis XIV was a very good dancer being 'instructed in this art' by the brilliant dancer and teacher Charles Louis Beauchamp, who became responsible for the choreography in the opera-ballets produced by Lully and the comedy-ballets produced by Molière. He even partnered the King himself and dressed as a girl, danced with him in *Le Triomphe de l'Amour* when it was presented at court in 1681. This opera-ballet is a land-mark because later it was the first to be presented before the public, and it was then danced by the first professional lady dancers, the leading danseuse being Mlle. Lafontaine. Hitherto the parts had always been played by the Queen and her ladies, members of the Royal Family and the courtiers. When it was shown publicly some of the courtiers had to be given special permission by the King to appear for there were not enough professional male dancers. The King himself did not dance in public.

The introduction of professional dancers had come about through the founding of an academy of dance. This had first been suggested in 1661 and some thirteen dancing masters met to discuss 'the raising of this art of dance to its perfection'. But they failed to agree and it was not until 1672 that Louis XIV commanded 'his beloved servant Jean-Baptiste Lully' to form an Academy of Dance within the Académie Royale de Musique. It still exists within the walls of the Paris Opera.

Jean-Baptiste Lully, an Italian, entered the King's service as composer of the King's Dance music in 1653 and quickly succeeded as composer, conductor and dancer. His gift for creating attractive dance suites for the court ballets drew greater attention to the musical side of the entertainments. These began to change, particularly when Lully introduced a new kind of performance, an *opera-ballet* in which singers played a more important role than the actors had done in the old *ballet de cour* and in fact took an equal part with the dancers. Such entertainments had been brought to Paris by Italians and were inspired by the first operas staged originally in Florence. But Louis XIV required Lully to transform these entertainments, to make them more French and thus more suitable to his grand court. More attention had to be paid to the spectacle and dance, and not so much to the words. In a very short time Lully made *opera-ballets* so popular that the King's advisers agreed they should be presented to the public and this led to the public production of *Le Triomphe de l'Amour*.

Some Characters in Ballet

In addition to the *opera-ballets* produced by Lully and Beauchamp, the great French dramatist, Molière had brought his company of actors to entertain the court and he shared his theatre with a group of Italian players known as the Commedia dell 'Arte. These players were descendants of the Dorian Mimes who first travelled through ancient Greece when the great tragedies of authors like Aeschylus were performed in the enormous theatres in honour of the gods. These mimes had no theatre. They merely set up a stage whenever and wherever they found an audience. They finally travelled all over Europe and because they mimed, danced and worked as acrobats, tight-rope walkers and the like, language was no problem. They also included plays about ordinary people and situations containing local gossip and news. Each member of the group was responsible for playing a particular part. The plots were hung up back-stage and each player knew the ways and habits of the character he or she played. In the 16th century these groups became known as the Commedia dell'Arte and were often the servants of some noble lord. Molière was fascinated by their methods and began to use some of their mime and dance scenes as interludes in his comedies. These interludes were later to develop on the one hand into the *ballets d'action* as we know them today, and on the other into the Harlequinades of the English theatre. When they worked in Paris with Molière they were very popular and greatly admired. Some of their characters and ways of dancing and miming are still part of our favourite

Above: Mark Silver makes his début as Oberon at the Students' Matinée

Below: Margot Fonteyn and Michael Somes as the Serious Lovers or *ballerina* and *danseur noble*

older ballets. From this source have come such favourite dancing characters as Harlequin and Columbine in Fokine's *Carnaval*, Franz and Swanhilda in *Coppélia* and Lise and Colas of Ashton's *La Fille Mal Gardée*.

But these were not the only characters brought by the Commedia dell'Arte firstly into Molière's *comèdie-ballets* and later into the *ballets d'action*, because dancers playing certain types of character still have to undergo the same strict discipline of the Commedia dell'Arte players.

1. The Serious Lovers

These are now the noble characters like Prince Charming and Princess Aurora in *The Sleeping Beauty* or the *danseur noble* and ballerina dancing Siegfried and Odette-Odile in *Swan-Lake*. Such characters had and still have to learn to behave as courtiers, remember the manners and rules of precedence, how to ride, fence, hunt or go hawking; to play a lute, sing a madrigal and above all perform with dignity and grace the fashionable court dances as in *The Sleeping Beauty* and *Romeo and Juliet*. In the 16th and 17th centuries they spoke verse. Today they must dance with graceful ease and charm the difficult solos and *pas de deux* created by such choreographers as Petipa, Balanchine and Ashton.

The plots of the Commedia dell'Arte plays were often about the Serious Lovers. A young man falls in love with a young girl, or she falls in love with him. But her guardian, widowed mother or miserly father will not allow the marriage. Instead it is arranged for her to marry some rich, old, ridiculous or wicked man. However in most cases there is a happy ending because the comic servants (often lovers themselves) of the serious lovers are so cunning or stupid, playing such tricks, disguising themselves or delivering letters to the wrong person, discovering one or another person in the wrong place and generally causing such con-

Lydia Lopokova and Stanislas Idzikovsky as the Comic Lovers or
Harlequin and Columbine in *Carnaval*

fusion that in the end the young couple are united. Thus the
comic characters are perhaps the most active in making the
plot work.

2. The Comic Servants or Lovers

The comic servants at the end of the 17th century became
known as Harlequin and Columbine and later grew more
important than the Serious Lovers. Audiences want
laughter as well as sorrow, which was often the fate of the
Serious Lovers until the very end of the play. Moreover the
Comic Servants were easier for everyone to understand.
They represented ordinary people who could dance the
folk dances, sing the popular songs and, more excitingly,
invent spectacular steps. Not only did they become the best
dancers in the troupe, they were often the acrobats, tight-
rope walkers and jugglers. Harlequin and Columbine had
their origin in ancient Greek legend and myth in which, as
Iris and Hermes, they were the messengers of the gods and
both wore winged sandals. The later Columbine often wore
wings and Harlequin a hat with wings. Hermes was also
god of travellers and animals, which is why Harlequin
moved and still dances with great speed and cunning. He
often changed himself into an animal and among the many
steps Harlequin is supposed to have invented are those
called after animals like the *pas de chat, temps du poisson*,

The Waltz of the Mice in *The Tales of Beatrix Potter*, the EMI production
distributed by EMI Film Distributors Ltd

Michael Coleman as Jeremy Fisher in the EMI production *The Tales of Beatrix Potter*

sauts de carpe, and *ailes de pigeon*. Perrot, the choregrapher of *Giselle*'s dances was born into a family of travelling players and made his first stage appearance as a monkey at the age of four. Today there are all the animals in the film *The Tales of Beatrix Potter*.

3. An Old Woman

She could be the Serious Girl's old nurse, mother, god-mother, step-mother or elderly guardian. This part was always played by a man, one of the oldest traditions of the stage, which dates back to the time when first the Greek and then the Roman audiences no longer had any respect for their gods and began to make fun of them, Juno and Jupiter in particular. Juno was often shown as a bad-tempered scold, always quarrelling with and berating her husband, Jupiter. He was shown as a wicked old man with an eye for a pretty girl and therefore always in trouble with his wife. Audiences found it much funnier if Juno and Jupiter had a knock-about fight which Juno usually won. No woman was expected to play such a part so there gradually developed an actor-comedian who always played an elderly woman, one who still has a home in English pantomime and ballet as do the Ugly Sisters in Ashton's *Cinderella*, Mother Simone in his *La Fille Mal Gardée* and Sir Frederick Ashton himself as Mrs. Tiggy-winkle in the film *The Tales of Beatrix Potter*.

Left: Sir Frederick Ashton as Mrs Tiggy-winkle

Right: Stanley Holden as Mother Simone in *La Fille Mal Gardée*

Anthony Dowell as Drosselmeyer with the children in *The Nutcracker*

4. The Old Man

There are several kinds of old man descending from the Commedia dell'Arte who are still found in ballet. Drosselmeyer in *The Nutcracker* is one of them. Such old men can be mysterious, sometimes acting a magician or an absent-minded scientist like Doctor Coppélius in *Coppélia*. They can be rich and wish to get richer still by wooing a girl with lots of money, or on the other hand like Father Thomas in *La Fille Mal Gardée* they can buy a wife for a simpleton son so that she will be capable of running his farm. In other ballets the old man has become an evil magician able to change those in his power into different shapes like Von Rothbart in *Swan-Lake* who transforms Odette into a swan; or like the Showman in *Petrushka*, who is in complete command of Petrushka's life and locks him in his cell except when he needs the puppet in the theatre.

Jesters in Scottish Ballet

Wayne Sleep as Puck in *A Midsummer Night's Dream*

5. Clowns and Fools

Many different types of clowns and fools have existed since the earliest days of the theatre. They play very differently. Three amongst them still have a place in ballet to supply laughter.

The first kind of clown are those wonderful dancers like Harlequin, who perform very difficult leaps, *pirouettes* and other exciting steps. The Jesters of Ashton's *Cinderella* and all Soviet productions of *Cinderella* and *Swan-Lake* do this. They are a little like Mercutio in many versions of Prokofiev's *Romeo and Juliet*, who makes fun of those who taunt him, jokes with his friends and still finds time to laugh even when he is dying. From this type of clown has also come ballets in which jokes are made in dance. For example, the Blue Boy in Ashton's *Les Patineurs* after dancing brilliantly, has to travel backwards and leans too far back in his excitement, so falls off stage. Or there are Jeremy Fisher, the Mice and other animals in *The Tales of Beatrix Potter*, who dance Ashton's fantastically characteristic steps. Their dancing all follows on directly in the tradition of a famous Harlequin, John Rich, who used to play Mother Goose in pantomime.

The second type of clown is the yokel, clumsy and boastful yet having a bit of an imagination. He is one of the most lovable characters in Shakespeare's *A Midsummer Night's Dream*. Bottom the Weaver 'had a most wondrous dream' that he fell in love with Titania, Queen of the Fairies. This dream was brought about by Oberon who sent Puck to find the herb 'the juice of which, on sleeping eyelids laid will make or man or woman madly dote upon the next live creature that it sees'. If ever you see Ashton's *The Dream* and the quarrels that Puck brings about because he sprinkles this juice on the wrong eyelids, and how Bottom, when changed into an ass dances *sur les pointes*, remember that Puck is like Harlequin, servant of the serious lover Oberon. Puck has therefore to show himself a cunning, clever dancer, Oberon a typical *danseur noble* while Bottom is the perfect example of clown.

Alexander Grant as Bottom

The third type of clown is that sad figure representing the ordinary little man for whom nothing ever goes right. He may be like Pierrot in Fokine's *Carnaval* who only wants one kiss and when he believes he has caught the girl of his dreams, finds that, like a butterfly, she has escaped. This type of clown may also be a simpleton or as they used to call him, a Zany. He is really a very sad figure like Alain in *La Fille Mal Gardée*, when he finds that no matter how magnificent he looks in his new clothes, white gloves, top hat and enormous buttonhole, he cannot marry the girl with his beautiful diamond ring. But at least he has found his red umbrella!

The saddest clown of all is found in Fokine's *Petrushka*, struggling to get out of the room in which his master imprisons him. He wants to find the Wax-doll he loves, and when he bursts through the door, finds the stupid girl dancing with the equally stupid Blackamoor who only wants to eat her. The Blackamoor however chases and appears to kill Petrushka with his great big sword. But even though the Showman persuades the crowd these dancers are only puppets, as night draws on Petrushka, the sad clown, suddenly appears on the roof of the puppet theatre as if to say: 'No! I am not dead yet. Whilst there is still a theatre and an audience, I will come back'. So all these characters from the past still come back for us to enjoy their dance and mime in many other ballets I have not yet mentioned.

Vaslav Nijinsky as Petrushka

Alexander Grant as Alain in *La Fille Mal Gardée*

Margot Fonteyn in the Royal Ballet's *Swan Lake*

The Australian Ballet Company in *Raymonda*

The Birth of the Ballet d'Action

The interludes performed in Molière's plays were not a new idea. Shakespeare had used mime scenes, the most important being the Players' Scene in *Hamlet*. There had also been mime scenes in many older mystery, miracle and morality plays and in the magnificent Masques produced for Elizabeth I and other English monarchs, as well as such wealthy nobles as the Duke of Devonshire. Such mimed scenes were often presented because the words were too difficult for ordinary folk to understand and they were sometimes played by the English Morris Men, who performed specially designed dances.

It is mime scenes like that in Shakespeare's *Hamlet* which historians have called the first *ballets d'action*, in which no word was spoken or sung to tell the story. Instead the dancers themselves had to do this. This kind of brief scene was presented as one item in a series of sixteen nights' entertainment given for one of Louis XIV's daughters, the Duchesse du Maine, in her palace at Sceaux in 1708. In it the dancers, Mme. Prévost and Mons. Balon, mimed a scene from *Les Horaces*. a play written by the great French dramatist, Racine. A sister sets out to find her brother, who

The Duchesse du Maine

has departed for the Crusade. Disguised as a knight, she meets and challenges another she believes to be a Saracen. They fight to the death and when their helmets are removed, it is discovered that brother and sister have killed each other. This tragic story was also used for a ballet by Skibine called *Le Combat*.

This scene probably counts as the first *ballet d'action* because it was the first time such a mime was performed by professional dancers trained by Beauchamp and his colleagues at the Académie Royale de Danse. Hitherto only actors with a special gift for mime, like that of the present day Frenchman, Marcel Marceau, had attempted this kind of acting. But Mme. Prévost was not only a fine dancer and mime, she was also a great teacher, two of her pupils, Marie Camargo and Marie Sallé becoming rival stars in 18th century Paris. And even if the English critics did not think much of Mons. Balon's talent as a mime when he visited London in 1712, he did have that wonderful gift of appearing so light that he bounced like a ball as he danced. We still call this gift after him, *ballon*, and many dancers work hard to acquire it and envy those who have it naturally.

When the English writer, Addison, criticised Balon's total lack of expression, it focused attention on dance as a means of communication. His criticism appeared in *The Spectator*, the important literary journal and John Weaver, dancing-master of Shrewsbury Grammar School replied to it in a letter explaining how dance at all times had been a means of conveying meaning. How David had danced before the Ark; Salome before Herod; how different people had danced and why they danced. Perhaps they wanted to ensure a good harvest, a happy life after a wedding; to express sorrow after a death; to worship their gods. Such dances have a place in ballet today. Nijinska's *Les Noces* and Fokine's *The Firebird* show two different kinds of wedding ceremony, the former among peasants, the latter of a Prince (the Tsarevitch) and a Princess. The various versions of Stravinsky's *The Rite of Spring* show peasants performing rituals in honour of their gods. Juliet dances tragically over Romeo's dead body. In ballets like *Petrushka*, *Rodeo*, *Coppélia*, *Pineapple Poll* and *La Fille Mal Gardée* we see stage versions of dances still performed by the peoples of the U.S.S.R., the U.S.A., Hungary, Poland and England.

But Weaver did more than just write about dance having meaning. He produced the first *ballet d'action* in which the dancers had to tell the story through movement alone. This was *The Loves of Mars and Venus* staged at the Theatre Royal, Drury Lane in 1717. It told how 'the great god Mars fell in love with Venus, goddess of beauty and how the jealous Vulcan captured them in a net forged by the Cyclops. But after other gods, goddesses and Cupid had pleaded for mercy, Vulcan forgave them'. Because Weaver was not sure that the audience would understand what the dancers were trying to say, he wrote a programme describing the plot and all the dances and the gestures the dancers would perform. We still use some of these gestures in older ballets. They are called conventional gestures. For example, if you want to say you are in love, open both arms outwards and sideways as you face the one you love, draw your right hand inwards and place it on your heart, then draw your left hand on top of the right and sway your body gently from right to left.

Svetlana Beriosova in the Wedding in *The Firebird* and as the Bride in
Les Noces, a peasant wedding

An African ritual and the Chosen Maiden in *The Rite of Spring*

The Parts of a Ballet d'Action

Weaver also worked out how to construct a *ballet d'action* containing the four distinct types of movement into which many older ballets are divided and which some choreographers still use. These are:–

1. *Scènes d'action*. In these the dancers tell some part of the story by conventional gesture without any dance at all. For instance in *The Sleeping Beauty* when King Florestan asks the Master of Ceremonies what he is hiding behind his back and why the four peasant women are being punished. He is shown the spindles which have been banished from the palace.

2. *Pas d'action*. These are dances in which some part of the story is told during the dance. During the Rose Adage in the same ballet when Aurora dances with the four Princes, each of whom wants to marry her, they ask her to dance with them, then express their love by presenting her first with a rose-bud and finally with a fully blown rose to tell her how deeply they have fallen in love.

3. *Variations*. These are the dances by which the heroes, heroines and other important characters in a ballet describe something about themselves. The first time Aurora appears she is very happy. It is her birthday and she wants everyone to enjoy her party and her movements express her feelings. The second time she appears it is as if she were dreaming of the day when a prince will come and waken her. The last time is when the Prince has kissed her and she is now ready to marry him and command her kingdom.

4. *Divertissements*. These are dances which sometimes have nothing to do with the plot but add more dancing to the ballet. For instance, at Aurora's wedding there are some specially attractive dances by the Blue-bird and Princess Florina, Red Riding-hood and the Wolf, Puss in Boots and the White Cat and other fairy-tale characters from Perrault's *Contes des Fées* the collection from which Aurora's own story is taken.

Weaver also realised that the dance music then fashionable was not suitable for his *scènes d'action* so decided to employ two different composers. Mr. Firbank, a dancing master wrote 'the dancing airs' and Mr. Henry Symonds, a member of the King's band of musicians wrote the 'symphonies' accompanying the mime scenes. This division of the music into that used for dance and that used for gesture was followed later by such important composers as Adolphe Adam (*Giselle*), Tchaikovsky (in all his ballets), Stravinsky and others. Weaver, like many later choreographers, could spend little money on scenery and costumes but we do know he tried to get rid of some of the heavy costumes then worn. As Venus Mrs. Hester Santlow, wife of the great actor Edmund Booth, 'danced with her hair loose and her skirt kilted up to her knee'. But despite all his efforts Weaver had to admit that not all his dancers 'were equal to his demands'. His choreography was unlike any they had danced before. Le Grand Dupré, the first soloist of the Paris Opera came to play Mars. At home he only danced the most elegant and slowest of dances, but as Mars he had to perform a 'Pyrrhic', a kind of war dance that is still performed by certain Morris dancers and by Greek soldiers, in which they practise sword play. Dupré also performed as Harlequin in a dance specially arranged for him by an English dancing-master.

Camargo and Sallé

Although Weaver's idea that dancers should tell their own dramatic or comic tales in *ballets d'action* grew popular in London, it only spread slowly through Europe. Most theatres were owned by royalty or wealthy noblemen who were mainly interested in showing off their learning and riches by staging spectacles to rival those of Louis XIV. Their audiences, particularly those in Paris, admired the magnificent costumes and scenery and the fascinating music of Lully and later Rameau. They were intrigued by the brilliant dancing of Marie Cupis de Camargo, pupil of Mme. Prévost, who led the ballets. She possessed remarkable *ballon* and could perform all the quick beaten steps hitherto danced by men. To display her swift neat footwork she shortened her skirts and lowered the heels of her shoes to make the beats easier to perform. Having been trained at the Académie Royale de Danse she quickly rose to the top, becoming a great favourite at court and was thus in an excellent position to prevent any rival taking her place, although there were other charming dancers like Marie Allard and equally fine male dancers.

Marie Sallé, who ultimately became Camargo's rival, was a different kind of dancer. She was born into a family of travelling players and when she first danced in London at the age of ten with her brother, she did not perform the elaborate versions of court dances like Camargo. Instead she stepped out in lively character or expressive dances such as 'The Dutch Skipper's Dance' or a 'New Harlequin and Columbine'. She was then working for John Rich, a famous Harlequin who staged both comic and dramatic *ballets d'action* following Weaver's example. When Sallé was sixteen she played the leading role in Rich's most successful ballet, *Apollo and Daphne* when, we are told that 'she learnt her art of speaking through dance from the English Harlequins'. The Italian actor who wrote those words introduced *ballets d'action* at his theatre in Paris, where, after the dancers had been taught mime by a Dutch dancing-master, they were staged by an Englishman called Roger. Sallé was not allowed to appear regularly at the Paris Opera, despite the efforts of Mme. Prévost to persuade the director that her two pupils, Camargo and Sallé, were so different in style that they would complement each other, and despite Sallé's success when she did make an appearance there.

Sallé worked very hard in any theatre where she could find a job and such was her artistry that she soon became a star. As her fame grew she became her own choreographer and put into practice Weaver's ideas that every emotion, mood and action can be expressed in dance. Her most famous ballet, *Pygmalion* (1734), tells 'how the sculptor, Pygmalion fell in love and brought to life the statue,

La Camargo

goddesses and great heroes from the stage and using instead common peasants and work-people. Such dancing would surely ruin the elegant technique of their aristocratic stars. But in 1789, when the French theatres were thrown open to everyone these new heroes and heroines were more popular because they appeared to behave and move in a way that the audience understood. *La Fille Mal Gardée* was soon being danced everywhere.

Once Dauberval had shown that ballets could be made out of everyday happenings, choreographers began to look everywhere for new plots and, as this new kind of *demi-caractère* dance developed, so ballets based on famous novels, plays, poems, contemporary events and sometimes original plots were staged. Although Weaver produced the first *ballet d'action* in England, his ideas were passed to France and then on to Austria, Russia and Italy; and although many dancers still went to Paris for training and to appear at the Opera if invited, they eventually either returned to their own countries, or found work in the ever increasing number of European theatres producing ballet.

Galatea he has created'. Sallé is said to have appeared as the statue in the lightest of Greek tunics, bare-footed and with her hair loose, something that had never been seen before in Paris. Another example of the popularity of Sallé's dancing was seen when Handel, the great composer, invited her to appear in his London seasons. For one of these he composed a special scene to open his opera *The Faithful Shepherd*. It was called *Homage to Terpsichore* in which Sallé appeared as the goddess of dance and had an overwhelming success.

Jean Dauberval

I wonder, when you watch *La Fille Mal Gardée*, if you realise it is the second oldest ballet in the repertoire? Do you know that its story comes from ancient Greece? The music too is old, but John Lanchbery brilliantly arranged these French tunes for Ashton's ballet. It is about 'a rich farmer who buys a wife for his stupid son, but finds the wedding cannot take place because the pretty girl's true love is found in her bedroom'. Such farming folk are still found in countries where marriages are sometimes arranged and even where *La Fille Mal Gardée* is performed. The choreographer, Jean Dauberval was the first to make them the heroes and heroines of a ballet and to design a type of dance we now call *demi-caractère*. In it you use the rules of your dancing lessons from your feet to your waist, but with your arms and head try to show what kind of a person you are and what kind of work you do.

Jean Dauberval produced his ballet in Bordeaux in 1789, the year of the French Revolution. He had been sent there because the directors of the Paris Opera felt his ideas, like those of his teacher Noverre and other learned friends, were too revolutionary. They thought he would ruin the effects of their great spectacles by driving their gods,

Jean-Georges Noverre

It was in one of Sallé's ballets that Jean-Georges Noverre first appeared. This French teacher, ballet-master and author is known as the 'Reformer' of ballet. In his book *Letters on the Dance* written in 1760, he says that dancers must do away with all the artificialities of court and *opera-ballets* if they are to tell stories by their own expressive movements. They must get rid of their heavy masks, wigs and costumes. They must perfect their technique, make their dancing appropriate to the rôles they play, dance to expressive music and not use the old fashioned court dances which expressed nothing but the steps. Their costumes and scenery must help the audience to understand where, when and how the plot develops. Only by doing all these things would dancers be able to play out the moods, emotions and actions of their characters as people do in real life.

Like Sallé, Noverre was not a pupil of the Académie Royale. He had to find work wherever he could and danced for Sallé in her *corps de ballet* before starting his career as ballet-master. But for all his wishes to change the face of ballet, he seldom put his ideas into practice. He usually produced great spectacles demanded by patrons like the Empress Marie-Thérèse of Austria who wanted her court to be as great as that of France. In Vienna Noverre rose to fame, particularly after he had visited London and worked for David Garrick, the English actor. He had been advised to come to England by that great French author, Voltaire, who had himself spent some two years studying the English ways of life, laws and arts. While in exile he realised, like many other writers of his time, that the arts must break away from the strict rules laid down by learned men if they were to be enjoyed by everybody. After seeing Garrick act in Shakespeare's plays and listening to English composers, Voltaire firmly advised the composer Gluck and then the ballet-master Noverre 'to go to England where they understand the beauties of Nature and use them to inspire their arts'. Gluck returned from London to Vienna and composed his ballets *Don Juan* and *Sémiramide* for the ballet-master Angiolini. Both were very successful, particularly the latter in which the leading dancer was Mdlle. Nancy, an Englishwoman, whom we are told: 'Had learnt to speak through the dance'.

It was for Mdlle. Nancy that Noverre staged his most dramatic ballets when he worked for the Duke of Wurtemburg in Stuttgart, now the home of the exciting Stuttgart Ballet (which was directed by the late John Cranko from 1961–73). At this opera house Noverre had the services of a large orchestra, his own costume designer, and a large company of dancers led by Gaetano Vestris, the star of the Paris Opera, who was only too happy to work for him. In Stuttgart Vestris could dance and mime dramatic rôles and not merely perform the virtuoso steps required when he danced at home. Yet despite Noverre's ideas that 'all nations and all peoples of the globe' should have a place in ballet, when he finally achieved his ambition of becoming ballet-master at the Paris Opera, he confessed 'that only noble characters doing noble deeds' were fit subjects for this great theatre. Eventually it was Noverre's pupils who changed the face of ballet, bringing all types of people on to the stage, introducing this innovation in the same year as the French Revolution, when at last the theatres were thrown open to everyone.

Charles Didelot

By the beginning of the 19th century ballet had become an important part of entertainment, particularly when the girls began to dance *sur les pointes*, which made a clear distinction between male and female dance. This method of dancing was introduced by another of Noverre's pupils, Charles Didelot, who also added simple lifts and began further to define the difference between steps for boys and steps for girls. He first did this when producing his ballet, *Zephyr and Flora* in 1796, in which the gentle wind fell in love with Flora, goddess of flowers and flew off with her to Olympus.

Didelot, who danced the part of Zephyr was short and not very handsome, although his technique was brilliant and as elegant as that of any *danseur noble*. Mme. Rose, his wife danced the part of Flora and her height and style was very like his own, therefore he worked on steps that suited his own powers of elevation, making his leaps look higher and he enhanced the light quality of his wife's dancing by sometimes lifting her from the stage in order to give the impression that the wind was wafting her into the air. He also used a new method of flying invented by the mechanics at the King's Theatre, London. This enabled Zephyr to lift Flora in his arms and apparently to fly not only across the stage, but also round in circles. Flora, too, was suspended on a wire during each flight, so she appeared to be running on her toes each time she left and returned to earth.

Didelot's most important work however was to lay down a firm syllabus for teaching dance at the famous school in St. Petersburg – now Leningrad. This school had been founded by the Frenchman Jean-Baptiste Landé in 1738 after he had been teaching the sons of Russian noblemen 'the delicate art of the Court Dance'. The story is that he came off the boat, saw some peasant children dancing on the quay and was so impressed that he finally persuaded the Empress Anne to let him start a school for the children of the court serfs. When Didelot arrived in 1801 dancers from this school were playing important parts in the court ballets as well as in the serf theatres owned by wealthy princes all over Russia.

Didelot found the pupils of the Imperial St. Petersburg Theatrical Academy studying all the theatrical arts so that if wanted they could sing in the operas, play in the orchestra, act in the plays, dance in the ballets, write out the parts for the musicians or actors and even work the scenery. But he changed all that. He realised that the success of his own and Noverre's ideas for ballets, depended on training dancers

Charles Didelot

capable of expressing themselves. Not only did they have to perfect their technique, but they had to learn to express themselves through suitable music, thus interpreting the parts they would play and conveying the meaning of the stories to the audience.

When Napoleon invaded Russia Didelot, being a Frenchman, had to leave, but returned after Napoleon's defeat and began to stage very different ballets using dancers he and his own pupils had trained, and who were now ready to interpret very dramatic rôles. He produced such ballets as *The Prisoner in the Caucasus*, inspired by Pushkin's poem and *The Hungarian Hut* inspired by a true incident in the life of Count Rakoczy, the famous Hungarian patriot who, when fleeing from the Austrian Army after leading a revolt against the Empress of Austria, was shielded by a young Hungarian Peasant girl. This last work was considered far too revolutionary by the Russian Tsar and Didelot was sent into retirement. His place was taken by Jules Perrot, whose choreography for the heroine's dances in *Giselle* is still performed.

Chapter 3
New Ideas in Ballet

Didelot's *Zephyr and Flora* in 1796 introduced other changes which would take place during the 19th century. The Industrial Revolution altered the life of many people and influenced all the arts. New inventions, like Didelot's flying machine, paved the way for other choreographers, who experimented with the newly invented gas, and later electric, lighting to produce more magical effects than candles and oil lamps, particularly when sylphs, wilis and the like danced silently in the moonlight during such ballets as *La Sylphide* and *Giselle*. Steamships and trains made travelling easier and faster so that leading choreographers and dancers could take their ballets further afield. But the Industrial Revolution also brought with it the toil and grime of factories, ship-yards and mines, making life much harder for those who worked in them. Rich industrialists took over the powers of the old aristocracy, who were now no longer able to act as patrons and employ great artists like servants to work exclusively for courts and imperial theatres. Moreover the artists themselves were seeking greater freedom to interpret the world of the imagination. They wanted to express their own spiritual and artistic ideas their own way and not be ordered to create this or that by wealthy and often uninformed patrons nor made to stick to strict academic rules.

The new search for inspiration was part of the Romantic movement which you should study later if you want to interpret and dance in ballets like *La Sylphide* and *Giselle*. In these the hero seeks a perfect love, but cannot find her in the world of the flesh, that is among his friends. Instead he finds her in the world of the spirit or his imagination. This same idea inspired Berlioz's *Symphonie Fantastique* which Massine turned into a ballet (1936) and Ashton's *Apparitions* (1936). Neither the musician (in the first) nor the poet (in the second) could compose or write until he had taken drugs. Then he dreamt that he saw and danced with his Beloved at a ball, in the country, elsewhere and finally at a Witches' Sabbath, where she eluded him for ever as he died at her feet. In *La Sylphide* James, a farmer, falls in love with a fairy and follows her into the forest forgetting his earthly fiancée, Effie, Count Albrecht falls in love with the peasant girl *Giselle* forgetting his wealthy fiancée Bathilda. But neither hero gains his heart's desire. James is cursed by Madge, a witch whom he has driven from his farm. In revenge she gives him a magic scarf with which to

capture *La Sylphide* and when he does so, her wings fall to the ground and she dies. Albrecht turns away from Giselle when Bathilda arrives with a hunting party. The simple peasant goes mad and dies. But when he shows remorse, so true is Giselle's love that she rises from her grave and saves him from being danced to death by the Wilis, before leaving him as the cock crows and all ghosts return to their graves.

Strangely enough it was Didelot who introduced such fairy-like creatures and witches to the ballet. He was very impressed by Shakespeare's 'magical scenes' and in *Flore et Zephyre* and other ballets tried to make his *corps de ballet* appear like the fairies in *A Midsummer Night's Dream*. He also borrowed ideas from the Witches' Scene in *Macbeth*. In one of his ballets his witches actually brewed a magic potion like Madge and her cronies do in *La Sylphide*. It was similar fairy- and witch-like creatures who took over the stage from the peasants and farmers of *La Fille Mal Gardée* when Marie Taglioni began to rise to fame with her first appearances in Paris.

Marie Taglioni (1804 – 1884)

Marie Taglioni was the daughter of an Italian ballet-master, Filipo, whose ballets were well-known in Western Europe. But his greatest success was his teaching work which proved how only strenuous and long training can produce a star. He turned his daughter, Marie from a thin, slightly hunch-backed, plain girl with long arms and legs into the most expressive and lightest dancer of the Romantic period. Many tales are told of how he worked Marie and her brother Paul until the blood flowed and she collapsed from exhaustion. But he strengthened her feet and ankles until she could finally poise on the tips of her toes, and when she made her Parisian debut it was this poising *sur les pointes* that astounded all the dancers and audience. Moreover when she appeared as a ghost-like nun in Meyerbeer's opera, *Robert the Devil* and later in Didelot's *Flore et Zephyre*

Scottish Ballet's *La Sylphide*

her extremely light and high elevation made her appear with her partner Jules Perrot: 'as if a puff of wind had swayed them . . . and they would soar forever upwards'.

Marie Taglioni's dancing at the Paris Opera inspired the leading tenor, Nourrit to write the story of *La Sylphide* (1832) to display her particular talents. The sight of this delicate fairy floating through the trees and running without leaving any footmark on the dew-spangled grass was to change and make more difficult the classical technique you now study. Once Taglioni danced *sur les pointes* no other dancer could appear without emulating her example. Her fame grew with each new ballet created specially for her by her father, brother and others, and each brought yet another fairy-like heroine on to the stage.

If you look at the many prints of Marie Taglioni, you will perhaps understand something of her genius. See how softly and expressively she rounds her arms and how delicately she holds the flowers. Note how easily she uses her head and eyes to indicate the line of her dance and the fond way she glances at the sleeping James. Look at the daintily pointed foot and remember her shoes were not strengthened and stiffened as they are today. Yet she could run as swiftly and poise as steadily on the tips of her toes as any of today's ballerinas. Such expressive dancing needs long years of work and practice.

You should also note the costume Taglioni wears. *La Sylphide* introduced the 'ballerina' skirt we still use in romantic ballet. No one knows who designed it. But it was a stroke of genius. It is like a 'ghost' of the dresses worn by the fashionable ladies of her period. Its low-cut bodice and misty sleeves revealed the shoulders and soft white arms. Its full skirt disclosed dainty ankles, feet and legs seen dimly through the transparent gauze as *La Sylphide* floated and ran soundlessly in the flickering gas-light. The simple wreath of convolvulus made her seem part of the fairy-world of a Scottish glen when contrasted with the gay tartans worn by James and the peasants.

Scottish Ballet's *The Witches*

The Qualities of a Dancer

You can still see *La Sylphide* produced by many companies. The most interesting version is that danced by the Royal Danish Ballet in Copenhagen where it has been performed ever since Auguste Bournonville returned from Paris in 1836. He had gone to study with Vestris and became soloist at the Opera and the King's Theatre, London before returning home. Once home he produced his version of *La Sylphide* and finally founded the famous Bournonville school, which has made so many Danish dancers famous.

Bournonville was a brilliant dancer himself, excelling in *batterie* and steps of *elevation*. He had a happy personality and most of the thirty-six ballets he created, many of them still danced, are full of the liveliest and gayest dances for soloists and *corps de ballet*. He was a magnificent but strict teacher and earlier in this book in the section about The Rules of Classical Dance (page 22) you have read what he required from his students if they wished to reach stardom.

Marie Taglioni in *La Sylphide*

Pas de Quatre

Pas de Déesses

Carlotta Grisi as Giselle

You should compare his wishes with what teachers look for if you go for an audition to a professional school. Bournonville wrote about these qualities towards the end of his life, long after Carlo Blasis had written his valuable *Code of Terpsichore*, giving us so many important rules of dance (see page 20). Later, of course, Bournonville's pupil, the Swede Johannsen brought his teaching to Russia. Then Diaghilev brought his Russian dancers to Europe and with his ballets changed the whole face of 20th century ballet.

1. Fanny Elssler (1809–1889)

Marie Taglioni was not without rivals. Her father's teaching of more expressive arm movements to suit his new fairy ballets was added to the strict technical rules insisted on by such famous dancing masters as the Vestris' father and son and the two Gardel brothers. This new training resulted in many *danseuses* trying to emulate the delicate art of Taglioni because most choreographers had to follow fashion and produce ballets like *La Sylphide* if they were to find work. But not all the new *danseuses* were so successful when appearing as a fairy, wili, naiad or ghost. Fanny Elssler's fiery temperament and energy were so different to those of Taglioni that the French writer, Gautier called her a 'pagan dancer' and Taglioni a 'christian' so pure and innocent she seemed in the rôles she played.

Fanny Elssler was born into a family of Viennese musicians and with her sister, Thérèse as partner, became famous, later travelling alone through Europe and America. Although she attempted Taglioni's rôles when she became star at the Paris Opera, her dancing was very different. She excelled, as Camargo had done, in brilliant *batterie* and very fast steps, often *sur les pointes* in which intricate patterns were made by quick changes of *épaulement* to show off her dark beauty and elegance. Her greatest successes came when she introduced a type of *demi-caractère* dance, the so-called Spanish *La Cachucha* and Polish *Cracovienne*. The excitement of both these dances lay not only in her tempestuous personality, but also in the rhythms she beat out by her brilliant playing of the castanets, or the dainty clicking of her heels together in the tiniest of boots.

It was Thérèse Elssler who first appeared dressed as a man to partner her sister. They danced in harmony as they had since childhood when they worked for a famous group of Austrian child dancers. But Thérèse's appearance *en travesti* – that is, dressed as a man – was followed by other girls as this novelty grew more and more popular until the male dancers, who had hitherto played a major rôle at the Paris Opera, gradually disappeared. By the time *Coppélia* (1870) was produced, the leading rôle of Franz was played by a woman. This remained the case until Lifar took over the Paris Opera ballet after the death of Diaghilev in 1929, when he insisted that men should play a leading if not the leading part in the ballets.

2. Carlotta Grisi (1819–1899), Jules Perrot and Giselle

Giselle (1841) is perhaps your favourite ballet as it is of many people. It is a great test for any ballerina. It can prove that she is not only a dancer of great lightness and delicacy, but also an actress. She must convince you she has been crowned Queen of the Vintage because she is the best dancer. She must show she is utterly sincere because when

Jules Perrot

she falls in love and that love is rejected, she loses her reason and dies. But her love is so true that when the Queen of the Wilis commands her to dance Albrecht, her lover, to death, she is so strong that she can sustain her ethereal dance until the cock crows and thus save him as she disappears into her grave. She must change from an earthly peasant knowing human feelings in the first act and in the second, must become a spirit knowing only deep love yet having enough strength to sustain her flowing dance until daybreak without ever seeming tired.

This rôle was made for Carlotta Grisi, a young Italian discovered by Jules Perrot, the choreographer whose work on *Giselle* (1841), *Ondine* (1843), *Esmeralda* (1849), *Pas de Quatre* (1845) and other ballets did so much to develop the art of the *danseuse*. He was a pupil of Vestris who had taken on the rather ugly nine year old boy from a circus for the sake of outstanding talent. Vestris arranged for his début at the Paris Opera, where he danced with Marie Taglioni, but was not given a permanent contract. Perrot began to tour, successfully teaching and producing ballets throughout Europe. It was in Naples that he found Carlotta Grisi

Antoinette Sibley as Giselle

Nadia Nerina and Konstantin Sergeyev as her Albrecht when she danced in Leningrad with the Kirov

and, after working to perfect her artistry, brought her to dance at a Parisian theatre. Here she was seen by the French writer, Theophile Gautier. He fell in love with her and her dancing, and persuaded the director of the Opera to engage her, first in an opera, when she was partnered by Lucien Petipa, brother of the famous choreographer and then in *Giselle*.

Giselle was a triumph. It was the work of four men all of whom loved Carlotta Grisi, the simple girl whose exquisite dancing, in their eyes, surpassed that of all others. She was able to express the deepest as well as the happiest of emotions and was equally convincing as an earthly peasant or a fairy sprite. Her particular qualities lent unusual drama and sincerity to all her movements. The four men involved in *Giselle* were Gautier, who roughly sketched out a plot based on a legend told by the German poet, Heinrich Heine, about the Wilis, the ghosts of girls who die before their wedding and rise from their graves at midnight to dance to death the lovers who have betrayed them. He gave this sketch to Count Vernoy Saint-Georges, already an expert at planning operas and ballets, who wrote his libretto in two scenes. The first represents the world of the flesh in which Albrecht tells Giselle of his love, but rejects her when his fiancée arrives. She goes mad and dies. The second represents the world of the spirit, when Albrecht prays for forgiveness and Giselle rises, like a ghost from her grave to save him from the anger of the Wilis.

Adolphe Adam, the composer of many operas and ballets created a score for *Giselle* quite unlike any that had been written before. He linked the dances of Giselle by compos-

ing five short musical phrases, one or the other being heard each time she is about to, or does, dance. They do not always sound quite the same because, as the story unfolds, these short passages change to help the dancer playing Giselle and her audience to understand how events can alter a person's moods, emotions and actions. These musical phrases are called *leit-motifs* and similar *motifs* were used by other great composers of ballet like Delibes, Tchaikovsky and Stravinsky to help other dancers and audiences to understand their ballets and characters.

Most of the dances in *Giselle* were arranged by the chief ballet-master at the Opera, Jean Coralli, although those we see now were mostly designed by Petipa for the Russian production. But Giselle's own dances were created by Perrot and are still danced. They are unusual. Each of Adam's *leit-motifs* is matched by a brief *enchainement*. These *enchainements* are repeated, but like their musical accompaniment, they change slightly each time they are danced; firstly by the happy peasant girl; then by the girl deeply in love; then by the tragic, mad figure before she dies and finally by the ghost-like Wili, whose flights through the air seem unearthly and insubstantial.

Giselle was not the only ballet Perrot created for Grisi. When he worked at Her Majesty's Theatre, London, he produced *Esmeralda* (1844), which is still danced in Russia, where he worked from 1848–59. It is based on Victor Hugo's novel *The Hunchback of Notre Dame*. This also displayed Grisi's two styles of dance. She first appeared as a simple gipsy girl with her goat, dancing and begging for a living and then in exquisite classical style as a Greek nymph in a *pas de deux* given to entertain and celebrate the betrothal of Fleur de Lys and the knight Phoebus, who has loved and then forsaken Esmeralda.

Left: Alicia Markova, the first English Giselle

43

Esmeralda was not only notable for the dramatic dancing of Grisi. It was the first ballet in which every member of the *corps de ballet* had to play an individual part in the scenes taking place in the market held under the arches of the Cathedral of Notre Dame de Paris. Before *Esmeralda* these dancers had usually been regimented into lines, mostly all dancing the same steps at the same time or forming figures like soldiers on parade. But Perrot wanted the scenes to look like real life and so he gave everyone something different to do, thus showing later choreographers how to give animation to the stage, as Fokine did in *Petrushka*, where his crowd at the Lent Fair on the frozen Neva behave like crowds do anywhere when out to enjoy themselves on a public holiday.

Margot Fonteyn as Ondine

3. Fanny Cerrito (1817–1909)

Perrot was also largely responsible for the success of Taglioni's third rival, Fanny Cerrito when she danced in London in 1843 in *Ondine*, a ballet which he created specially for this charming, plump little Italian. She became almost as famous as Taglioni, although her style and temperament were very different. She was warm-hearted, lively and excellent in strong allegro, that is fast dances. Yet Perrot created for her one of the most poetic of all solos, almost rivalling Anna Pavlova's *The Dying Swan*. This dance was called *Pas de L'Ombre*, or Shadow Dance, and was performed when Ondine, the water-nymph, leaving the water, first saw her shadow and danced with it. There are several prints showing this dance. But perhaps you may see the film of the beautiful dance created by Ashton for Margot Fonteyn in his version of the old story of the water-nymph 'who learns to love a mortal, who,

although he loves her, loses her in a storm and marries a mortal. But Ondine's master, the King of the Sea takes his revenge and floods the prince's great castle, drowning the betrayer of his beautiful nymph'. If you see the film watch how Ondine plays with her shadow as it grows shorter, then longer and sometimes disappears. Nowadays the lights needed to create this effect are easily found, but in Cerrito's day it was very difficult to find one gas lamp that would give enough light to show the dancer's movements, but not so much that it lost the effect of her shadow as she danced. No wonder that the audience applauded the magical effect of the dance.

4. Lucille Grahn (1819–1907)

Taglioni's fourth rival was the Danish dancer, Lucille Grahn who created the rôle of *La Sylphide* when Bournonville produced it in Copenhagen. Although slim, tall and blonde with ethereal, light yet strong movement, many considered her a cold dancer. Others admired her strength, wonderful elevation and proud dignity. Perrot created *Catarina, Daughter of the Bandit* and *Lalla Rookh* or *The Rose of Lahore* specially for her, believing that her talent lay in *demi-caractère* and not romantic parts. Certainly the London newspapers writing about these ballets when first produced admired her Sicilian and so-called Indian dances where she displayed earthly characters rather than imaginary. Nevertheless she did manage to be convincing in romantic rôles, although she does not seem to have had quite the same flowing movements as her rivals.

Perrot chose these more dramatic ballets like *Lalla Rookh* and *Esmeralda* for Lucille Grahn and Carlotta Grisi because he wished to show London that tragedy too had a place in ballet. He knew it had been proved at La Scala, Milan where the choreographer Vigano believed his 'dancing Tragedies' based on Shakespeare's *Coriolanus* and *Othello* as well as one called *The Titans* about the downfall of the Greek gods, were more important than all the great spectacles presented in the State and Imperial Theatres throughout Europe.

The Pas de Quatre (1845)

Yet despite their rivalry four of the greatest dancers of their day did appear together in a *divertissement* created for them by the choreographer with whom they had all danced and for three of whom he had composed successful ballets. That such an event as the *Pas de Quatre* with choreography by Jules Perrot and starring Taglioni, Grahn, Grisi and Cerrito could be staged at Her Majesty's Theatre, London, a capital city without a ballet of its own, is strange. But not so strange when you discover that it was suggested by no less a person than Queen Victoria that the event should take place and be organised by the manager of the theatre, Benjamin Lumley. He always tried to bring before his audiences the greatest stars of opera and ballet he could persuade to cross the Channel and he worked in this theatre for some twelve years. These four dancers had all appeared

for him and Perrot had staged some very successful ballets and similar *divertissements*. So to crown his 1845 season, Lumley brought all five together. The marvellous collaboration between such deadly rivals was due entirely to Perrot's deep understanding of each dancer's particular talent. He arranged their solos so that each was seen to the greatest advantage, performing those steps best suited to her particular style, and when they danced together neither one nor the other was given pride of place. Taglioni finished centre with the others grouped round her because she was the oldest.

The *Pas de Quatre* was reconstructed by Keith Lester for the Markova-Dolin ballet in 1936 and since then has been revived several times notably by Anton Dolin. Although we cannot be certain that the steps are performed exactly as they were in 1845, at least we can see the difference between the styles of these four dancers as well as something of the Romantic ballet to which they all belonged.

Arthur Saint-Léon and the Character Ballet (1821 – 1870)

It was not only the new steam trains and ships that led to dancers travelling round Europe and America. The 19th century was also the time of wars and revolutions which often made them escape from the battlegrounds to more peaceful cities. You will remember how Didelot, a Frenchman, had to leave when Napoleon invaded Russia in the last of his attempts to conquer Europe but returned to produce his most interesting ballets after the Emperor was defeated. The 1848 French Revolution drove dancers away from Paris and this event marks the point when the Opera ceased to be the most important European centre for ballet. Other great cities like St. Petersburg, London and even New York were attracting more and more famous dancers and choreographers.

This travelling to foreign countries greatly influenced the work of many choreographers. Bournonville had, of course, introduced dances that he had learnt abroad when he returned to Copenhagen. Didelot had introduced Georgian Cossack dances into *The Prisoner in the Caucasus* and Dauberval used Provençal and Basque dances in *La Fille Mal Gardée*. But like Fanny Elssler's *La Cachucha* and *Cracovienne*, these were not true folk dances. They were performed in soft ballet slippers or dainty boots, like those worn when dancing the courtly *Mazurka* and *Czardas* in *Swan-Lake*. However the movements in the latter have far stronger national characteristics than those in Bournonville's *Napoli* (Italian) and *Far From Denmark* (Spanish). His dances were based on classical steps with *demi-caractère* arm movements to give a recognisable style. You know how Scottish dancers hold their arms in *The Highland Fling* and Spaniards used their bodies, heels and castanets.

The dances in *Swan-Lake* look more genuine because of the work of the dancer and choreographer Arthur Saint-Léon. This lively man, son of a touring ballet-master, called himself 'a Jack-of-all-trades'. He danced well and partnered such great dancers as Taglioni, Grahn and Cerrito in Perrot's *Pas de Déesses* for the 1846 London season. This little ballet was based on the story of Paris awarding the golden apple to the nymph he most preferred. But Saint-Léon was also ready to produce a ballet suitable for the dancers and theatre in which he worked. He could compose the music because he played the fiddle well and in fact actually played it himself when dancing the leading rôle in his ballet, *The Violin of the Devil*. He was prepared to make do with costumes and scenery from the theatre's own stock if money was short and to work for nothing but his fees as a dancer. If his plots did not please, then he would change them to suit the wishes of the director of the theatre.

Yet despite his willingness to conform, Saint-Léon did a great deal to bring character ballet to the stage – the kind of ballet, like *Coppélia*, which uses a stage version of folk dance to make the story seem more real.

Saint-Léon's first effort at such a ballet was *The Little Humped-Back Horse* produced in St. Petersburg in 1864. He had taken on the job of ballet-master there after Perrot retired and for some time was successful in producing the same ballets he had used in Europe. But the Maryinsky Theatre audiences got tired of seeing ballets that resembled or were repeats of others given under different titles. Luckily Saint-Léon had a very good friend in the editor of an important St. Petersburg newspaper, who suggested it might be a good idea to make a ballet from the favourite Russian folk-tale *The Little Humped-Back Horse*. 'This magical horse comes to poor Ivanoushka's help whenever he is in trouble and cracks a magic whip she has given him. He is sent by the Khan to find the Tsar-Maiden. But when Ivanoushka brings her back, she refuses to marry the Khan unless she is wed with a magic ring. So Ivanoushka is sent out again through earth, air, fire and water to find that ring. But when Ivanoushka brings it back, she refuses to marry unless the Khan regains his youth by bathing in boiling asses' milk. The Khan orders Ivanoushka to try the bath first and he comes out as a handsome Prince. The Khan simply cannot wait, plunges in and, in a cloud of steam, disappears forever. Ivanoushka marries the Tsar-Maiden'.

Saint-Léon put everything he knew into this ballet. To music by Cavos, the Italian composer of Opera and Ballet at the Imperial Theatres, he staged a multitude of dances. If ever you see the Soviet version, there are exciting dances from many parts of Russia, for the birds of the air, rushing fire and underwater scene where every possible fish, coral and sea-weed take part. Finally the tiniest shrimp, played by a pupil of the Moscow Choregraphic School, brings Ivanoushka the magic ring.

Coppélia was Saint-Léon's last ballet and is based on one of the strange *Tales of a Nutcracker* by E. T. Hoffmann. They are told by Godfather Drosselmeyer to his god-daughter Clara who is in bed after a serious accident. He has previously given her for her birthday a wonderful mini-ature house full of mechanical dolls, which she loves, and she comes down one night to find a great rat chewing her favourite doll. In her fright she breaks the glass and cuts her arm so badly that the shock and injury make her very ill. Drosselmeyer therefore comes to help her pass the time with his *Tales of a Nutcracker*. These tales also serve as plots for Offenbach's opera *The Tales of Hoffmann* and the Tchaikovsky-Ivanov ballet, *The Nutcracker*.

Hoffmann wrote his tales when the first mechanical dolls were being made and people began to wonder if such automata would ever be given life like the creatures you read about in science fiction today. Many people in the ballet world found it a fascinating subject and Saint-Léon, with the help of Nuitter, a lawyer who worked out the librettos for many Parisian operas and ballets, set out the plot we now use.

Coppélia is set in Galicia in Poland, which at that time was part of Prussia. This gave Saint-Léon a chance to introduce some lively Polish dances and customs into the tale of how Franz neglected his sweetheart, Swanhilda, to woo Coppélia, a mechanical doll made by Doctor Coppélius. When Franz steals into the workshop he is caught by the old man, who drugs a glass of wine before he gives it to Franz to drink to their friendship. Coppélius then tries to 'magick' the life out of Franz and give it to his doll. But Swanhilda has taken the place of the doll and after pretending to come to life, she finally succeeds in waking Franz. The couple disappear happily leaving a broken-hearted Coppélius with the ruins of his beautiful doll'.

When you study the history of music you will learn how opera and ballet music was changed when certain composers broke the Italian and French rules for creating such works. Instead they turned for inspiration to the folk music of their own countries. The five Russian composers known as 'The Mighty Little Heap' are among the best-known and their music became famous when Diaghilev first brought Russian music, opera and ballet to Europe. Delibes, who wrote the music for *Coppélia* was not a national composer in the same sense, but whenever he wrote a score for an opera or ballet whose plot was laid in one particular country, he was careful to use some of its special sounds. For example when he composed the opera *Lakhmé* set in India, he made his orchestra sound like temple bells and gongs, and when he wrote his score for *Coppélia*, he borrowed tunes from a Polish opera for his *Mazurka* and the dance for Swanhilda's friends. He added a typical Hungarian *Czardas*, a dance tune then becoming popular because of the playing of Hungarian Gipsy Orchestras, which gets its name from the *czarda*, or village inn before which the villagers dance on Sunday nights. Delibes also gave a Scottish and Spanish flavour to the dances when Swanhilda pretends to be the doll.

It is not known whether the dances in today's *Coppélia* were arranged by Saint-Léon. It is doubtful, for the ballet has seen many changes since it was first produced in 1870, just before Saint-Léon died. Nevertheless he made certain rules for staging character dances on the stage.
1. Only use the most typical steps from any one country.
2. Emphasise the special arm or foot movements such as the squatting steps of the Russians, the pointing of toes of the Scots and the playing of castanets by the Spaniards.
3. Arrange the dance so that all the steps are seen best from the audience's point of view. No one wants to see

nothing but the dancers' backs and most traditional folk dances face in towards the centre of a circle.

4. Pay great attention to fitting the steps to the music. For example, English country dancers step down on the beat, whilst Highlanders spring upwards.

The part of Swanhilda was originally to have been danced by Adéle Grantsova, one of the first Russian dancers to appear in Paris, but she had to return to St. Petersburg before *Coppélia* was ready. The delay was because Saint-Léon, who was ballet-master of St. Petersburg, Moscow and Paris had too much work and simply could not travel such distances to rehearse. Finally it was produced by the French ballet-master Mèrante and its success was due to the delightful dancing of Giuseppina Bozacchi. This seventeen year-old Italian was a brilliant technician and her lively personality suited the rôle of Swanhilda. Her Franz was Eugénie Fiocre, known for her beauty. This playing of a boy's rôle by a girl was typical of the time, when not only were there few male dancers but those that existed had been recruited into the Army to fight in the Franco-Prussian War. In addition, neither the management nor the audience of the Paris Opera were in any way interested in male dancers.

Marius Petipa (1819–1910) and Classical Ballet

'*The Sleeping Beauty* is a pearl of great price'. So wrote a Russian critic about Marius Petipa's masterpiece. It was his last important ballet and is still the one which best displays a ballerina's command over technique and uses the classroom steps at their most perfect. It is the one classical ballet still danced which demands that everyone in it has complete control over her movements and dances in harmony with the music. Next time you watch it see how each step flows into the next. See if you can understand how Petipa divided them into seven different categories. These are:–

1. *The Preparatory Steps* which take you from one pose, *pirouette*, beat or jump into the next.
2. *Petit and Grand Elevation* are all kinds of jumps allowing you to travel upwards, over, along and round the stage so that not only the ground is covered with movement but also the air.
3. *Petit and Grand Batterie* are all the beaten steps both large and small which make your dance sparkle and show how quickly your feet and legs can work.
4. *Ports de bras* are the flowing movements of your arms without which your dance is meaningless.
5. *Pirouettes* are all kinds of turns which can make your dance exciting, particularly if you suddenly change direction, or spin many times in place.
6. *Poses.* There are many times when you pause for a

moment to allow the audience to look at the pose you have made and make them understand why it has a place in the dance. It is rather like looking at a photograph, which can be studied in detail and looking at a film where movements are continuous and sometimes difficult to appreciate fully.
7. *The Pointes* or the steps you dance on the tips of your toes and give the finishing touch to your dance.

Marius Petipa worked for the Imperial Theatres for nearly sixty years. He first came as a soloist and assistant to his father, Jean, who was appointed ballet-master in 1847. But the ballets they produced were not very original and the audience became tired of watching works they had seen elsewhere. The Maryinsky Theatre audiences were largely made up of diplomats and wealthy Russians who travelled widely. Many were attached to the court and frequently visited cities such as London, Paris, Vienna and Milan. However, although Jean Petipa's contract was ended, Marius stayed on and gained the title of 'Soloist to the Tsar'.

As a soloist he worked under Perrot and then Saint-Léon learning all he could about production and choreography and from time to time he staged a ballet of his own. Just before Saint-Léon died, Petipa was appointed chief ballet-master and began to have some success. He had made friends with the same editor who had helped Saint-Léon. But this time the suggestions were inspired by events happening in the world and the librettos were often written by that master of planning, Count Saint-Georges, who wrote *Giselle*. It is rare that we have such ballets today, although some choreographers try to use items of news, just as Catherine de Medici did when she tried to unite the people of France when she staged *Ballet Comique de la Reyne*.

Some of the ballets that Petipa staged were suggested by items of interest to the fashionable world. *The Daughter of Pharaoh* (1862) was based on a novel by Gautier, inspired by the excavation of the Egyptian Pyramids. It is about a rich English traveller who seeks shelter from a storm in the pyramid. He smokes opium and has a most fantastic dream about Pharaoh's favourite daughter whom he rescues from a lion and other wild adventures follow. The ballet contains one scene in which five of the famous rivers of the world, the Guadalquiver, Thames, Congo, Neva and Tiber with their tributaries dance the national dances of the countries through which they flow. Another ballet, *Le Roi Candaule* (1868) with libretto by Saint-Georges was about the warrior king Gyges of Lydia, whose palace had been recently excavated. Yet another was produced when the river Scheldt, which flows through Holland into the North Sea froze over in 1879. It was called *The Daughter of the Snows*.

The list of Petipa's ballets seems endless. But despite their variety, the Maryinsky audiences got bored because the stories were usually lost in masses of dances which had little to do with the plot. Even the dancing of the great stars Petipa brought from Paris and Milan failed to keep them interested. These stars were mainly interested in showing off the difficult steps they could do *sur les pointes*. The new methods of teaching started by Taglioni and Blasis were having an effect, and their legs and ankles were so much stronger. Moreover a little stiffening was being added to the back of their shoes and across the toe-piece.

By 1888 the Director of the Imperial Theatres thought of sending Petipa away, the audiences were not coming to the theatres. But he decided he would give Petipa one more chance. The director himself, Count Vsevelozhsky was a learned man and loved ballet. He decided *The Sleeping Beauty* would be an excellent subject to display Petipa's great knowledge of classical dance and the talents of many Russian soloists – Petipa's own pupils since he became head of the school in 1855. He also felt that if he could persuade Tchaikovsky to compose the music all would be well because the composer was at the height of his fame. After some persuasion Tchaikovsky agreed but only if he were given all the necessary details. His first ballet, *Swan-Lake*, had not been successful when staged in Moscow because the ballet-master there had not given him any help. Vsevelozhsky then persuaded Petipa to write the full libretto. This is fascinating to read. Petipa wrote down everything. The kind of music he wanted, its time-signature and tempo, the number of bars, sometimes the instruments he felt were best suited and how one tune must flow into the next. In addition he made notes to help Tchaikovsky understand what was happening on the stage. For example this is how he describes the Lilac Fairy giving her gift to Aurora after the Wicked Fairy Carabosse has told the King and Queen that their daughter will die if ever she pricks her finger.

> 'The good fairy bows before the cradle: "Yes, you will fall asleep my little Aurora as your sister Carabosse has willed" says the Lilac Fairy. "But not forever. A day will come when a Prince will appear who, enraptured by your beauty, will plant a kiss on your forehead and you will wake from your dream in order to become the beloved wife of this Prince and live in happiness and prosperity."'

Tchaikovsky was inspired by such instructions and wrote, as he told his brother, 'some of my best music'. Certainly Petipa created his finest dances to that music. In them he put into practice all he had ever learnt. From Blasis came the laws of balance which you see used beautifully when Aurora poises in *attitude* in the Rose Adage and each of the Four Princes in turn takes her hand and turns her round. From Bournonville he learnt how to study the particular talents of each soloist and from Perrot how to give them the steps they perform most perfectly.

But Petipa was not only interested in the dancing. He made notes of how to change the scenery and give the illusion of the magic boat travelling down the river of dreams; how to make props and to use mechanical devices like the trap-door in the stage through which Carabosse disappears. Nothing was left to chance and although he did not design the scenery and costumes, he made sure they were as he wished.

The ballet was and still is a success. The only thing it lacks are dances for men. Petipa was not interested in them. He even forgot to give the Tsar's soloist any dance at all until the wedding, and then only because Paul Gerdt, playing the Prince, insisted. The beautiful Blue-bird's dance was arranged by Enrico Cecchetti then aged forty and famous at that time not only as a great classical dancer, but

Anthony Dowell as the Prince in *The Sleeping Beauty*

also as a mime. He played the Wicked Fairy, Carabosse, the same part he played at the age of seventy-one when Diaghilev produced *The Sleeping Beauty* in London in 1921.

Vsevelozhsky was so pleased with *The Sleeping Beauty* that he felt another ballet by Petipa and Tchaikovsky would also be a success. He decided to use Hoffmann's *Tales of a Nutcracker* and worked out a plot using several of them. One was about a battle between the toy-soldiers and sweets hanging on a Christmas tree and the rats and mice. Another was about a king-rat biting a baby princess and turning her into a horrible creature. Another was about Drosselmeyer and a friend going to find a young man who could crack a magic nut and save the princess. Yet another was about the young man who had been turned into a nutcracker. It was all very muddling and Petipa had great difficulty in sorting out the different ideas. Finally he worked out the story of *The Nutcracker* as we know it today.

In the first act Godfather Drosselmeyer brings gifts to Clara and her brother Franz at their Christmas party. Among these is a nutcracker which Franz breaks and Clara

Moira Shearer and Sir Frederick Ashton in the Royal Ballet's *Façade*

David Wall and Doreen Wells in the Royal Ballet's *Two Pigeons*

sadly puts it in her doll's cradle. When the guests have gone all is dark, Clara comes downstairs to see how her nutcracker is. She is alarmed by the cuckoo clock striking midnight and the rats scratching in their holes. The fir-tree grows enormous. At a bugle call the toy soldiers led by their captain go into battle against the rats. It seems as if the terrible Rat King is about to kill the gallant Captain. But at that moment Clara takes off her shoe and throws it. The toys and rats disappear and a handsome Prince appears. He invites Clara to come with him to *The Kingdom of Sweets*. Then Petipa tells us :–

'There is a change of scene to the Fir Forest in Winter.
Snow begins to fall. Suddenly a snow-storm occurs.
Light, white snow-flakes blow about (60 dancers).
They form snow-balls, snow-drift, but at a strong gust of wind, the drift breaks up and becomes a circle of dancers.'

In the second act Clara and the Prince arrive at *The Kingdom of Sweets* in which Petipa found a place for an endless variety of dances, chocolate, coffee, tea, marzipan, silver-balls, crystallised fruits and flowers and the like. They certainly all bow to Clara, but the Sugar-Plum Fairy comes to dance with the Prince, and by this time the story has completely disappeared. It is not surprising that poor Tchaikovsky faced with such a muddled plot wrote to his brother saying: 'Today, more than ever, I am finding it impossible to portray the Sugar-plum Kingdom'. He certainly did his best and some of the dances have become favourites for their lovely sparkle, interesting use of instruments and wonderful rhythms.

Lev Ivanov (1834 – 1901)

Before Petipa started rehearsals he fell ill so his assistant, Lev Ivanov had to undertake the choreography. He is the first Russian choreographer we have mentioned in our history although there have been others. But Ivanov's work has proved to be the most important of the late 19th century. Unlike Petipa who sometimes arranged the dances before he heard the music because he knew exactly what he had ordered, Ivanov had first to hear the music and then design his dances. When faced with *The Nutcracker* he had to try and follow Petipa's orders, but it was very difficult. He had to tell all the complicated story in the first act and arrange only a series of dances for the second and although some of these were very effective, the ballet as a whole was not a success.

Today there are several versions. That by Rudolph Nureyev tries to give you the idea that poor Clara after her accident is having nightmares and gets Drosselmeyer mixed up with the Nutcracker and the handsome Prince. This makes the ballet a little easier to understand.

However Lev Ivanov's greatest works are the two scenes of the Swans in *Swan-Lake*. As you read earlier, this was the first of Tchaikovsky's ballets and because it had not been very successful when produced in Moscow, the composer promised to re-write his music before it was produced in St. Petersburg. Unfortunately he died in 1893, before this happened, but at a concert given in his memory a year after his death Ivanov staged act II, or *The Flight of the Swans*. This was the success of the evening and the Tsar ordered that the whole ballet be revived.

Petipa and the composer-conductor Drigo got to work on the libretto and the music trying to turn it into Petipa's usual type of ballet with plenty of *divertissements*. But they found it too difficult to change the scenes of the Swans. Moreover the Tsar had decreed that Ivanov's work was not to be changed. Ivanov was therefore asked himself to arrange the last act when Siegfried comes to beg forgiveness. When you next watch *Swan-Lake*, see if you can understand the difference between the work of two choreographers, Petipa and Ivanov in the tale of a Princess, Odette. 'She has been captured and turned into a Swan by the wicked magician, Von Rothbart. Prince Siegfried, who is out shooting, sees her and falls in love swearing to marry her. But when he returns to his Palace, and his Mother insists he should choose a bride, Von Rothbart appears with his daughter, Odile. She so enraptures Siegfried by her cunning looks that he forgets Odette and chooses Odile for his bride. At this moment the magician and his daughter disappear. Siegfried, overcome with remorse at what he has done, rushes back to the lakeside and begs Odette's forgiveness. Von Rothbart tries to part them. But so strong is their love that he is vanquished. Odette and her Prince sail away on the river of dreams.'

As you watch the story unfold, you will perhaps understand how Petipa arranged some brilliant dances for his soloists – particularly for his ballerina in Act III, when Odile dazzles the Prince with her dance. Note particularly the famous thirty-two *pirouettes fouettés en tournant* and remember this was the first time such a step had ever been performed. It was danced by the Italian ballerina, Pierina Legnani. But when you watch Ivanov's two scenes of the Swans, first of all see how he makes Odette's movements seem like those of a swan, floating through the water, shaking its drops from her wings and head, and landing softly as if from a flight and craning her beautiful neck. Then you must listen to the music and try to understand how dancers and musicians must work together. In the beautiful love duet in Act II, you can get the clearest idea of how Ivanov makes his Odette's dance rise and fall with the melody and how the other swans sometimes echo her movement, whilst the orchestra echo the melody of the solo violin and cello. It may be easier to understand if I tell you what Fokine, Ivanov's great pupil once told me :– 'Listen to the music and let it tell you what to do'.

Chapter 4
Ballet in the Twentieth Century

Serge Diaghilev (1872 – 1929)

During the first ten years of the 20th century the whole idea of ballet was changed by Diaghilev, when he brought his Russian company to Western Europe and completely altered the old-fashioned ways of ballet-making. The first performances of *The Polovtsian Dances* from *Prince Igor*, *Les Sylphides*, *The Firebird*, *Petrushka* and *Spectre de la Rose*, and after the 1914–18 war, *The Three-Cornered Hat*, *Les Noces*, *Le Train Bleu*, *Apollo* and others, left his audiences astonished by the superbly expressive dancers led by Tamara Karsavina and Vaslav Nijinsky. The variety of tales told by the choreographers Fokine, Massine, Nijinska and Balanchine danced to strangely fascinating tunes and rhythms made everybody listen hard as well as look at the blazingly colourful costumes and sets by Bakst, Gontcharova and other important artists. People began to realise that these ballets were no longer made up of *scènes* and *pas d'action*, *variations* and *divertissements* like *The Sleeping Beauty*. The soloists did not just display their virtuoso steps. Everyone working in any one ballet, choreographer, composer, artist and above all the dancers had only one thought: 'The Ballet Itself'. Everyone had to make an individual contribution to the plot or theme and thus communicate its meaning to the audience.

Diaghilev was no dancer, artist or librettist. He did play the piano and thought of becoming a composer after he began to study law in St. Petersburg. Yet his love and knowledge of all the arts that go to make a ballet grew to such a degree that when he finally formed his company he understood perfectly which artists he must bring together to produce the very best results. All had to work in harmony to present a finished work, a ballet for which dance, music, set and costumes were specially created and could not be used in any other way.

Diaghilev learned all this in the course of many visits to his cousin's flat. Here he used to meet regularly with a group of men all interested in or practising the arts. At first he only listened to their discussions. But when they decided to start a magazine 'The World of Art' Diaghilev was made

editor, and he began to travel widely to study and to stage exhibitions. Later he edited the Imperial Theatre's Year Book which brought him into contact with the dancers themselves and with the young choreographer, Mikhail Fokine, whose new style of choreography was to inspire the world when Diaghilev enthusiastically decided he must show Russian Ballet to the West.

Mikhail Fokine (1880 – 1942)

Mikhail Fokine had been one of the most brilliant students of the St. Petersburg Theatrical Academy before he joined the Maryinsky Ballet as a second soloist. Two years later at the age of twenty-two he was promoted to first soloist and made teacher of the senior girls' class. With his students he began to put into practice ideas he later used in his ballets. He realised, as Didelot had done earlier, that if he were to re-awaken interest and throw out all the old ideas which only bored the audience, he must train dancers who would be ready to answer his demands. His methods of teaching were based firstly on co-ordinating every movement with music of the highest quality and secondly in making every movement of every dancer expressive in two ways. The first way he called mimed-dance, and in it you described your moods and emotions as you danced. The second way he called danced-mime in which, as you danced, you told your audiences how and why you did that kind of work or behaved in that kind of way.

Fokine produced his first ballets for his students and these were based on the vast knowledge he had gained when a student. He was deeply interested in both classical and folk music, playing the piano and balalaika. He spent hours in museums and art galleries sketching, painting and collecting information about dance, types of movement, scenery and costumes. He read world literature and the history of the theatre. All this study made him understand how to introduce reforms into ballet and soon after he began to teach he sent a letter to the Director of the Theatre summing up the changes he wished to make. From time to time he also wrote letters to newspapers setting out his ideas. By 1906, when he produced *Chopiniana* (re-named *Les Sylphides* by Diaghilev) and *The Dying Swan* both for Anna Pavlova, his ideas could be summarised thus :–

1. Dance in ballet is not a series of classroom *enchainements*. Instead it must express the characters the dancers are playing, the period and place in which they live and if necessary, their nationality. Each ballet must have its own exclusive style of dance.

2. Neither dance nor gesture have any meaning in ballet if they do not help to tell the story. He always believed the audience had no need to read the story on a programme. If they had to do so then he said the dancers and the choreographer were not doing their work properly.

3. The dancers must use their whole body to express meaning and use conventional gestures only if these suit the style and period of the story to be told.

4. All the dancers in a ballet, from the leading dancers to the most humble member of the *corps de ballet*, must be expressive. If their thoughts are right, their facial expressions will be right. These will affect all the movements of their bodies and if every dancer feels his or her part deeply, so will all the others on the stage. In this way the whole stage will be filled with expressive movement.

5. These new ballets will be ones in which choreographers, composers and artists will work together in complete equality.

But Fokine's letters and articles were ignored, although the Director of the Imperial Theatres allowed him to experiment with his pupils at their Graduation performances. His first ballet *Acis and Galatea* in 1905 marked the first appearance of Nijinsky and Lydia Lopokova both still students. In 1907 came *Chopiniana* and both these ballets were staged at a Charity performance. Wealthy patrons became interested in Fokine's work and often invited him to produce new works. One of these was *Carnaval* in 1910 and another, *A Night of Egypt*, later named *Cleopatra* by Diaghilev came in 1908. It should have been a magnificent spectacle, but the Director of the Maryinsky would not spend any money so Fokine had to make do with costumes and scenery borrowed from operas and ballets with an Egyptian setting such as *Aida* and *The Daughter of Pharaoh*. Nevertheless when Diaghilev re-staged it for his 1909 Paris season with costumes and sets by Bakst, the brilliant colouring and superb dancing of Anna Pavlova, Tamara Karsavina and Nijinsky created a sensation.

Fokine's most important ballet for the Maryinsky was *Le Pavillon d'Armide* in 1907. Benois, the artist, had based his three act ballet on a novel by Gautier, but whilst he was away Tcherepnin, the composer and conductor of the Maryinsky, and Fokine together reduced it to three brief scenes. It tells how 'A Vicomte spends the night in a magician's castle. He falls in love with the beautiful girl he first sees on a Gobelin tapestry. But alas the dream fades and he is left only with a scarf. He falls senseless.' Benois was furious at the shortening of his story, but Fokine's brilliant choreography astounded not only the audience but also the dancers. They realised for the first time how much mood,

Margaret Barbieri and Alain Dubreuil in *Les Sylphides*

emotion and action could be expressed through conventional gestures when they were made part of the *ports de bras* and were not mere signals to be used when standing still.

Le Pavillon d'Armide was only one of the ballets that demonstrated how Fokine was using traditional movements in a new way. Sometimes he chose themes from the romantic world and showed how *Les Sylphides* dance in a moonlit glade when inspired by the music of Chopin. They are not cruel like the Wilis in *Giselle*, but are dreaming of love like the Young Girl in *Spectre de la Rose*, who dreams that the spirit of the rose her partner gave her at her very first ball, comes to life and dances with her. In *Carnaval* Fokine showed a ball in full swing. Here couples meet, perhaps lovingly, gaily, shyly and even sadly. In other ballets he produced great spectacles as Petipa had done. But he never allowed the story to be lost in divertissements. In *Cleopatra* he arranged dances for Negro, Greek, Syrian, Egyptian and other slaves, but when the great Queen entered, all movement ceased while she cruelly parted the

Above: Sir Frederick Ashton as the Koschei in *The Firebird*

Below: Margot Fonteyn dancing the lullaby in *The Firebird*

two lovers Ta-Hor and Amoun, enticing the latter to her side. In *Scheherazade* with the most fabulously coloured costumes and sets by Bakst, you could see how Queen Zobeide waited until her Shah and his brother had gone hunting before persuading the Chief Eunuch to release her lover, the Golden Slave, and also the lovers of the other wives in the harem. Then at the height of the passionate dance, the Shah and his brother return unexpectedly and, with their soldiers, kill all who have disobeyed his commands, even his favourite wife, Zobeide.

However, Fokine's most exciting and important ballets were based on Russian folk and fairy tale, music, dance and art. *The Firebird* and *Petrushka* were created with Stravinsky as the composer and Golovin (later Gontcharova) and Benois as the artists. All were Russian born and it was their deep love and knowledge of the traditional arts of their vast country that taught choreographers everywhere that it is not enough to study the classical rules of any art as laid down by learned men for the glory of some rich court, like that of Louis XIV. Nor is it enough to find inspiration in the doings of ordinary folk as Dauberval did in *La Fille Mal Gardée*, although such themes will always find a place in ballet. Nor is it enough to find inspiration in the world of the spirit in contrast with the world of the flesh as the choreographers did in Romantic ballet. These Russian artists taught us that treasures are to be found in tales told and sung by generations of grandfathers and grandmothers to tiny children, to explain some wonderfully mysterious happening of the long distant past, 'The Once Upon a Time of an imaginary world where magic birds come to your help and puppets have a life of their own'.

I well remember my first sight of *The Firebird* flashing through the mysterious garden, the strange murmurs of wind and trees; how the Tsarevich climbed over the wall in the gloom and dropped silently to the ground. Again the

Michael Somes as the Tsarevich in *The Firebird*

Petrushka, the Fair on the ice

great bird flew through the air and disappeared. My excitement grew when she returned and was caught in the Tsarevich's arms. Why did she struggle so to be free? Why did she finally tear that magic feather from her breast, give it to him and fly joyously away? The strange music changed to a simple tune as a group of girls came through the trees. Although I had never seen such costumes before I knew they were Princesses so calm and dignified was their dance. Why did the most beautiful of them go to the tree and help shake down the apples? I soon understood for as they played and threw their apples to each other, the Tsarevich caught Hers, took off his hat, looked into her eyes and immediately fell in love, later taking her head between his hands and kissing her. Years later I learnt from Fokine that he had used a traditional wedding dance as the Princesses slowly drew the couple together for that magic kiss. But then I was frightened by a new sound, the Princesses ran away, the Tsarevich tried to climb the wall, but was trapped in the garden. He knocked at the great gates which opened, and the strangest assortment of creatures surrounded him. Finally came the Koschei, the oldest and most evil man I had ever met in my fairy tales. He was a skeleton in a bright coloured cloak and wonderful crown, whose long finger-nails terrified me as he cast a spell on the Tsarevich. But when the Tsarevich spat in his eyes, I felt

much better because my grandfather had always told me: 'Spit evil in the eye if you know you have done no wrong'. So when the Tsarevich waved the magic feather and the Firebird flew in I knew all would end happily. And so it happened on that night so long ago, and will happen again when you go and see this ballet. The Firebird dances her Lullaby and when the Koschei, his servants and the Princesses are asleep, she commands the Tsarevich to fetch the large box containing the Koschei's life in a large egg. He throws the egg, it breaks and all within the magic garden disappear as to the glorious tune of an old Russian Easter hymn the most beautiful Princess and the Tsarevich are married and crowned Queen and King surrounded by all the other Princesses and their bridegrooms.

Petrushka also fascinated me for although its first sounds were familiar, it became so different. Living near Hampstead Heath always meant that every Bank Holiday the family took a long walk to that liveliest of Fairs. Father and my brothers went to enjoy the swings, roundabouts and side shows. But because I hated crowds, I was left sitting high enough to see them until they came to take me to the real treat, the Punch and Judy show. To watch *Petrushka* meant starting with a world I knew, although I soon realised these Russians did not sing and dance like our Cockneys, and no English nursemaid would think of bringing her charges to the Fair, let alone allowing them to dance. But the sudden hush as the Charlatan came out of the theatre to play his mysterious tune immediately cast a spell over me. Why were Petrushka's eyes so sad? Why was the Doll so stupid and unkind? Why did the Blackamoor chase and kill so lovable and helpless a puppet? To me he was not a puppet and although he called and called for help, it seemed nobody but one nursemaid and me cared about him. I wept, as I still do whenever the dancer playing Petrushka speaks to me with his eyes as Massine did on that first visit.

Dancers for Fokine and Diaghilev

1. Vaslav Nijinsky (1880–1950)

No! I never saw the first and greatest of Petrushkas, Vaslav Nijinsky. Today his name is a legend for his dancing was remarkable in two ways. He was a brilliant classical dancer whose elevation made him look as if he hovered in the air each time he leapt. He was also a great artist and Fokine

Antoinette Sibley and Anthony Dowell in Jerome Robbins' *The Afternoon of a Faun*

created many rôles in which he could display his genius as dancer-actor. He could be the mischievous Harlequin, the dream-like Spirit of the Rose, the Golden Slave in *Scheherazade* and the tragic Petrushka. He made audiences realise how much ballet had lacked before Diaghilev and Fokine re-introduced the superb Russian male dancers led by this strange genius. But sadly his strangeness grew until he became lost in a world of his own, though not before he had tried to create some ballets himself.

Diaghilev soon realised that despite Fokine's great gifts, he could not create enough ballets to fill the repertoire. His company were now dancing three ballets at each performance instead of the one long spectacle which had been usual before Fokine showed that a short ballet could tell a story just as well. Diaghilev decided to turn Nijinsky into a choreographer. He took him to art galleries, museums, concerts, theatres and then, with the artist Bakst, suggested the only Nijinsky ballet you might see danced today, *The Afternoon of a Faun*. This was a strange ballet to come from a great classical dancer, in the same way that Robbins' version is a strange work to come from a choreographer who has done so much to stage real American ballets like *Fancy Free* and *U.S. Export, Jazz*.

Diaghilev and Bakst had been on holiday in Greece where the artist had sketched scenery and friezes of dancers seen round the pediments of ancient temples and vases. Nijinsky translated these sketches into movements, danced to Debussy's music. This had been inspired by Mallarmé's poem, 'The Afternoon of a Faun'. 'In the heat of a sunny afternoon a Faun lies dreaming of nymphs dancing before him. One is so beautiful he wants to possess her'.

Nijinsky's Faun and Nymphs forgot all about classical technique. They used neither turn-out nor *épaulement*. They moved as if dancing along a frieze in straight lines. Their *ports de bras*, seen in profile were very angular. Their dance was quite unlike any yet seen by audiences of that time – 1912. But when I first saw it with Massine as the Faun, it did not seem too strange. I was then dancing with Margaret Morris, having been very ill. She had had a classical training, but after seeing Isadora Duncan and having some musical study with Jaques-Dalcroze, she began to develop a form of Greek dance from the same sources that had inspired Nijinsky. It was from these people searching for a form of freer movement that the first modern dancers like Ruth St. Denis, Mary Wigman, Rudolph von Laban, Kurt Jooss and Martha Graham started to develop their own work and to free dance from the artificialities which had hindered dancers from expressing themselves. And from these groups most of the leading modern dancers and choreographers today, such as Glen Tetley, Paul Taylor and the new style Rambert Ballet have taken their inspiration.

Nijinsky's second work for Diaghilev, in 1913, was a disaster. This was *The Rite of Spring* to Stravinsky's music. If you listen to it now it does not seem strange, its wonderfully powerful rhythms may even make you want to dance like primitive peoples still do, stamping, leaping and hopping enthusiastically to the beat of their drums and tunes played on ancient pipes. But when the Parisian audience first saw and heard the ballet, they booed and the orchestra refused to play. *The Rite of Spring* was so unlike anything

Diaghilev had presented before. The dancing was not graceful like *Les Sylphides*, nor exciting like the *Dances from Prince Igor*. The costumes were neither colourful nor interesting. Why put a lot of clumsy Russian peasants on stage to practise an ancient rite in which the Elders of a tribe select a girl to be sacrificed to the gods?

Today there are many versions of *The Rite of Spring*. The Belgian Maurice Béjart, the Englishman Kenneth Mac-Millan and the two Soviet dancers Kasatkina and Vasilyov have created successful ballets. To me only one, the Soviet version, seems right because it brings out the atmosphere and rhythms of Stravinsky's marvellous score. It was, after all, composed by a Russian about Russians for a Russian company, who hear the music differently.

2. Tamara Karsavina b.1885
In spite of the beauty of that most beautiful of Princesses and all the other magnificent dancers in the Diaghilev company, it was *The Firebird* herself who stole my love and became for me the greatest of all dancers. Since then many other ballerinas have become favourites in this or another rôle. But Tamara Karsavina still remains the greatest story-teller of them all. How, I used to wonder, could she be the immortal Firebird, the gayest of Columbines, the cruel, yet beautiful Queen Thamar, the Young Girl dreaming of her Rose, the Miller's Wife in *The Three-Cornered Hat* and, or it seemed to me, a hundred different people? Later she taught me how much she had to study before living her part on the stage; how much discipline lay behind each step and gesture; how to phrase and dance to the music; how much make-up and costume helped or hindered her movements. We in London were so lucky she married an Englishman and settled here to give us so generously of her time and wisdom. The Royal Ballet owes her a particular debt for helping stars like Dame Margot Fonteyn and Nadia Nerina to reconstruct such rôles as *The Firebird* and Lise's scene in *La Fille Mal Gardée*, when, locked in by her Mother, she imagines what it would be like to be married to Colas, have three children and teach them to read.

3. Anna Pavlova (1881–1930)
Although Fokine created his first version of *Chopiniana* and *The Dying Swan* and other important rôles specially for Anna Pavlova, and although Diaghilev brought her to Paris as a leading star of his first season, she did not stay long with his company. It is difficult to understand why he did not persuade her to become part of his wonderful band of artists. Perhaps she was too much of an individual and did not enjoy being a member of a group of dancers with immense talent working under a choreographer, and being moulded into their parts. Perhaps she did not enjoy being directed by Diaghilev and Fokine, both of whom insisted that dances were danced as choreographers arranged them, that the dancers made up and wore costumes, wigs and shoes as the artist designed them. And the steps were danced to music, like that of Stravinsky, which in those days sounded strange and required much rehearsal.

We shall never know why she preferred to go her own way, forming her own company and – after she had made her home in England – filling it with English dancers who,

she found, were always willing to accept the strict discipline and exhausting tours she made all over the world. But if she had not danced so exquisitely everywhere she went, many of today's leaders of ballet might never have been inspired to start on their careers. Amongst the people she influenced are Dame Alicia Markova, Dame Margot Fonteyn, Sir Robert Helpmann and the foremost English choreographer Sir Frederick Ashton. Thus English ballet, perhaps more than that of any other country, owes much to this fragile dancer in whose Hampstead garden you can still see swans, whose beautiful movements are for ever associated with her most famous dance, *The Dying Swan*.

4. Leonide Massine b.1895
The outbreak of the 1914–18 War, followed by the Russian Revolution of 1917, brought many changes. These events made it more and more difficult to bring dancers and others from Russia. So Diaghilev turned his attention elsewhere. He had already begun to use composers and artists working in Paris and when he first arrived, his ballet became the centre round which they all circled. One of the last dancers he brought from Moscow was Leonide Massine, specially chosen to dance the leading rôle in *The Legend of Joseph* (1914). In the absence of Fokine and the failure of Nijinsky's ballets, Diaghilev believed his new dancer could become a choreographer and under proper guidance provide him with the new works he needed. And so it proved.

Massine had been trained both as a dancer and actor and had appeared in the Bolshoi ballet from an early age because of his extremely expressive face and striking eyes. He had a deep love of literature and music; both his mother, a singer, and his father, a musician, worked in the Bolshoi so when Diaghilev made him study at art galleries and museums and sent him to concerts and theatres he was already well prepared. He also worked under the great Maestro Cecchetti, whose daily lessons ensured that the classical technique of Diaghilev's dancers never suffered, even though few of his ballets depended on the strict discipline of the classroom exercises that one performed every day. Nevertheless Diaghilev and his choreographers believed, like all ballet-masters and choreographers of today, that classical dance is the firm base on which to build a company.

Massine learnt more than classical dance from Cecchetti. The Maestro and his wife were superb mimes, using the conventional gestures as if they were the most natural things in the world. The Maestro's performances as the Charlatan in *Petrushka* and the Chief Eunuch in *Scheherazade* made Massine realise how he could create characters with gestures suitable for the many different styles of dance he used. The infinite details of movement he first learnt from Cecchetti he now uses in his own expert system of notation.

Massine's first ballet was *The Midnight Sun* in 1915 a gay festival of Russian dance staged because of Diaghilev's patriotic feelings. But the Russian Revolution turned his attention to the artistic sources in Europe and his first idea came from Italy. *The Good-Humoured Ladies* in 1917 was based on a Commedia dell'Arte plot to music by Scarlatti, which Diaghilev himself chose for Massine. This lively ballet tells how an old Marquis and his wife, three pretty girls and their lovers are continually being mistaken one for the other because of the tricks played by the maid-servant and her lover, a waiter, who like Harlequin and Columbine, cause the utmost confusion before bringing all the right lovers together again. It was very funny and introduced Massine's clever way of so timing gesture and step that they make us laugh.

Diaghilev then celebrated the signing of the Versailles Peace Treaty in 1918 with Massine's *La Boutique Fantasque*, as if to demonstrate how many nationalities were involved. 'To a fantastic toy-shop on the Riviera come two English old-maids, an American and a large Russian family. The very continental shop-keeper and his boy with a running nose, display dolls from Italy, Poland and Russia, a mechanical melon-seller who jerks along and runs over an English Snob, two French poodles, one of whom misbehaves badly, and lastly two lovers, Can-Can dancers, whose antics shock the old maids. Sadly the lovers are sold to different families. But at midnight the other dolls come to life and release them from their parcels and when the shop re-opens, drive all the customers away in a mad Can-Can.' The two lovers were danced by Massine himself and Lydia Lopokova, who had already captured London audiences by her enchanting performance as the maid in *The Good-Humoured Ladies* and other rôles. Her lively performance as Swanhilda in *Coppélia* with the Sadlers' Wells Company in 1933 will never be forgotten. She was yet another Diaghilev dancer to marry and settle in London, where she and her husband, now Lord Keynes, worked so hard and so generously to help the newly formed English Ballet after the death of Diaghilev. It was his influence that secured the Royal Opera House for a performance by the group on February 23 1946, just after the war; and the group, now The Royal Ballet, lives on in this same beautiful Theatre.

Diaghilev's next inspiration came from Spain where he had seen an old story acted by mimes and set to music by Manuel de Falla from whom he commissioned a ballet score. He then persuaded the artist Picasso to design scenery and costumes. Meantime Massine had been studying the various styles of Spanish dance with a gipsy, Felix. Thus *The Three-Cornered Hat* displayed much of the sunny yet tempestuous life of the Spanish people. I believe it was, and still is, the best Spanish ballet in any repertoire. 'It tells how the old Corregidor orders his soldiers to take the Miller a prisoner because he wants the Miller's pretty wife. But the Miller escapes and not only makes fun of the Corregidor but also throws another of his wife's suitors into the river'. The story is told by a mixture of Folk and Flamenco dance. The latter is fascinating. It is usually performed only by Spanish gipsies who break into dance on the spur of the moment, and just as they feel. You are sometimes asked to do this in your dancing lessons. But Massine had to capture this feeling while disciplining the movements to fit the music, not like the gipsy, whose guitarist accompanies the dance and changes his tune as the dancer wills. Massine did what Fokine had done with Russian dance and used danced-mime. Thus as the dancers mimed such episodes as the Miller and his wife drawing water from the well, or teaching their canary to sing, they also danced. Massine danced the Miller and Tamara Karsavina his wife, and it was his wonderful solo, the

Farucca and her dance after he was arrested by soldiers that ensured the ballet's success. It also suggested to Diaghilev that Massine now had enough experience to restage *The Rite of Spring*.

I shall always remember that revival of *The Rite of Spring* for the outstanding performance of Lydia Sokolova as the Chosen Virgin. She had been the first English dancer to join his company and the rôles she danced for Diaghilev seem endless. She excelled in character parts, although when she danced her gay Columbine or her dreamy Sylphide, her classical dance became deeply expressive because she was so musical. Her greatest rôle was however the Chosen Virgin where she made you understand her fear yet reverence for the Elders, who chose her to be sacrificed. Never will I forget that tense figure as she remained stock-still, for ages it seemed, until with a tremor which shook her whole body, she met her fate. Despite this great performance, the ballet still did not interest the audience. The theme, the Stravinsky music, the Roerich costumes and scenery, were still too primitive, too unlike Fokine's fairy tales to which Massine had now added *The Midnight Sun* and *Contes Russes* about the witch, Baba-Yaga and her cat Kikimora. Massine too was tired. In the short space of five years he had created about ten ballets and several short dances under Diaghilev's personal supervision. He felt he must lead a life of his own, married one of the English girls in the company and was promptly dismissed.

Diaghilev's *The Sleeping Princess* 1921

Disappointed in the work of his next suggested choreographer the dancer Slavinsky, Diaghilev decided to fulfil a long cherished wish and stage *The Sleeping Princess* (why she was not called the Beauty as in Russia is not known). He hoped to show Europe the former glory of the Imperial Ballet which had been submerged, or so he thought, by the new Soviet government. This wonderful production at the London Alhambra was produced with scenery and costumes by Bakst, and brought on to the stage three of the greatest Imperial ballerinas, Lubov Egorova, Vera Trefilova and Olga Spessitseva, with the younger Vera Nemchinova and sometimes Lydia Lopokova to dance Aurora. The last named usually danced the Lilac Fairy as well as the Bluebirds, partnered by Stanislas Idzikovsky, yet another Diaghilev star to settle in London and share his experiences as a student of Cecchetti and a dancer under the major choreographers of the Russian Ballet. Pierre Vladimirov, the great *danseur noble* came to partner the Auroras before he joined Anna Pavlova. Even Carlotta Brianza the very first Aurora was persuaded to act as Carabosse, the wicked fairy for one exciting Gala. Finally there were a number of English dancers taking part, including Errol Addison, Anton Dolin (under the name of Patrikeff) and the late classical dance could mean. So that season closed and it looked as though the Diaghilev ballet would have to disband.

Diaghilev's Last Choregraphers

Nijinska (1890–1972) and Balanchine b.1904

However, the failure of *The Sleeping Princess* did not after all, end Diaghilev's activities. Every year since 1911 the company had presented a season in Monte Carlo. As they gave a few performances a week and sometimes also appeared in the operas, they could rest, take classes and rehearse new ballets. Here came wealthy friends ready to help Diaghilev with his money problems. He now called in Bronislava Nijinska, Nijinsky's sister. Nijinska had arranged several dances to music from *The Nutcracker*, which Diaghilev had added to *The Sleeping Princess* to give more chances to his male dancers. He had admired her wisdom as well as her classical dancing and had made her responsible for bringing to perfection the classical dances of *The Sleeping Princess*. This ballet had first been rehearsed by Nicholas Sergeyev, whose knowledge of the Russian system of notation later enabled the Sadlers' Wells Ballet to re-stage many of the other world-famous Imperial ballets like *Swan-Lake*.

Diaghilev realised the help Nijinska had given to her brother and she felt had something new to say. She produced what we now call her masterpiece, *Les Noces* (1923). This was Diaghilev's last attempt to create a Russian ballet based on traditional material, a peasant wedding danced to the strange rhythms and melodies of Stravinsky's score in a very simple set, with costumes by Goncharova. The artists responsible for *Les Noces* were all Russian born and were convinced that after the Revolution any colour in the life of the peasants was gone. All that remained was their passionate love of dance as they joined in their ancient *Khorovods* (circle dances). Today you can see the dancers forming beautiful groups round the Bride and Bridegroom who scarcely dance at all as they are the centre of the ceremonies. Perhaps you will enjoy, as I do, the singing of the ancient Russian rites and the fascinating rhythms as the guests all join in the final dance. But you may be disappointed like some of its first audiences were. It is not like Diaghilev's other Russian ballets. Nor is Stravinsky's music like that of *The Firebird* or *Petrushka*. But like *The Rite of Spring* it may make you want to join the dance. Moreover although Goncharova's costumes and set in brown, white and black have so little colour, their very simplicity shows up the strength of the gestures made and the dance patterns. This was an effect that a later artist, Sophie Fedorovitch, also achieved when she designed set and costumes for Sir Frederick Ashton's most beautiful ballet, *Symphonic Variations*.

Diaghilev's disappointment at the lukewarm reception for *Les Noces* was great. He now decided that he must supply

Anton Dolin, Diaghilev's English dancer

Ursula Moreton, later head of the Sadlers' Wells and Royal Ballet School – and of course Dame Ninette de Valois.

Seraphina Astafieva, another of Diaghilev's dancers, had also married and settled in London to open a school and at Diaghilev's invitation her students, of whom I was one, could go to any matinée, so we saw each Aurora in turn and compared our likes and dislikes as you do today. We were also anxious to see some of our older colleagues dancing in the *corps de ballet* and to know if Alicia Markova was really to dance as the youngest fairy (the authorities did not in fact allow it) and if Patté Boy (Dolin) was behaving himself! But *The Sleeping Princess* was not a success and had to be taken off. It had cost too much money and the audiences were not large nor were they interested enough to sit through a long ballet. They had been used to seeing three very different ballets presented by Diaghilev in one evening and the style and classical quality of *The Sleeping Princess* was not to their taste. It only became so much later, after Dame Ninette de Valois and the Sadlers' Wells Ballet had spent time and energy teaching English audiences what

Above: Vera Nemchinova and Serge Lifar in *Les Biches*

Left: Lydia Sokolova, also in *Les Biches*

Lydia Sokolova, Slavinsky and Lifar in *Les Matelots*

his wealthy audiences with what was fashionable, chic and daring. Everything was to be new for the sake of being new. This led to Nijinska's ballet *Les Biches* (1924). It told how a wealthy hostess invited The Bright Young Things (as debutantes and their boy friends used to be called) to a house-party. The girls gossiped and flirted with three handsome young men, who were more interested in showing off their muscles and fine figures, whilst the Hostess, with a fashionable gown, long string of pearls, cigarette holder and an enormous ostrich feather in her head-dress became, so she hoped, the centre of admiration. Georges Auric's music caught the popular rag-time rhythms and Marie Laurencin's set and costumes were like the pictures she painted to hang in fashionable ladies boudoirs.

The success of *Les Biches* (or The House-Party) suggested another idea. The story says that Diaghilev and Nijinska saw Anton Dolin enjoying himself on the beach. He was a fine swimmer and diver. We, Astafieva's students, also knew he could compete and beat us in doing cartwheels, handstands and other acrobatic feats, so we were not surprised when the antics of this handsome newcomer to the company suggested the idea of *Le Train Bleu* (1924). At this time it was fashionable to go to the Riviera on the famous Blue Train and enjoy yourself sun-bathing, swimming, flirting, and playing such games as beach-ball, golf and tennis. *Le Train Bleu* showed how society might have behaved – if they had been dancers. The train had arrived, the holiday makers, dressed in clothes made by the famous Parisian couturier, Chanel, were enjoying themselves as they danced and played to the new jazz-like music of Milhaud. The ballet was centred round Dolin's acrobatics and was thoroughly enjoyed by its Monte Carlo and Parisian audiences. But it is significant that when Dolin left the company, *Le Train Bleu* ceased to exist.

Nijinska was not happy with Diaghilev's continual interference with her work; she left and Massine returned to produce his new ideas. But instead of dealing with fashionable pursuits, his *Les Matelots* (1925) told how two ordinary sailors ashore, picked up a pretty girl and her friend to pass the time of day. Like all Massine's choreography the details worked out in dance were fascinating. Can you sit on a chair and play a game of cards with a friend when there is no chair or cards? Can you row out to sea with no boat or oars? Massine's Sailors did. Diaghilev even employed a street musician to play the spoons. He found this man entertaining theatre queues in Leicester Square, London, and remembering that playing spoons used to be common amongst sailors, felt it might stress how everyday things help a ballet. The idea opened up an entirely new field for later choreographers; it influenced Americans, like Agnes de Mille, who staged *Rodeo* and Englishmen like Walter Gore who staged *Street Games*. *Les Matelots* also used one idea which was very old. A huge cube stood on one side of the stage and on each side was painted a rough sketch – the waves, the outside of a tavern, some trees – and every time the sailors reached another episode in their day on shore they turned the cube around. This was like the *perakatoi*, or cube used in ancient Greek dramas. As the story unfolded so the actors turned the cube to reveal yet another sketch telling the audience more about the scene. This device is often used today.

Another new Massine ballet was *Le Pas d' Acier* (The Age of Steel, 1927) to glorify the age of the machine which Diaghilev felt was taking over artistic life. Somehow in this extraordinary work Massine made his dancers look like the cogs, wheels, pistons of a machine, particularly in the finale, when the scenery worked too and you felt you were looking at some enormous engine. Oddly enough the ballet set a fashion for chorus dancers in revues and musicals and Massine himself used the idea when arranging dances for the famous line of girls known as the Rockettes at the Roxy Cinema in New York.

In 1924 a small group of dancers from Leningrad, who had been allowed to tour Germany decided to try and join Diaghilev. They were led by Georges Balanchine and Alexandra Danilova, later to become a very important ballerina for many companies. Balanchine had studied to be a dancer, for the priesthood and also music, as his father was an important Georgian composer. He had also done some choregraphy and had worked under two Soviet choregraphers Feodor Lopukov (Lydia Lopokova's brother) and Kasyan Goleizovsky. They were experimenting with new forms of ballet in which they tried to interpret great music in terms of classical dance. The former had created one ballet to Beethoven's Fourth Symphony and the latter became known for his interpretation of music by Scriabin. When Balanchine later settled in New York and helped Lincoln Kerstein to found the School of American Ballet in 1933, he returned to their ideas – that dance itself is all that is needed in ballet. The long list of works he has since created which have no theme or story but are set to music by composers like Bach, Mozart, Tchaikovsky, Bizet, Hindemith, Bernstein and in particular Stravinsky, shows how wide is his musical knowledge.

But Diaghilev's first task for Balanchine was *Barabau* (1925) almost a political ballet. It told how a stupid officer, acting like a dictator, was outwitted by a cunning peasant woman. *The Triumph of Neptune* (1926) which followed was produced specially for Diaghilev's London season. But as I already possessed some of Pollock's Toy Theatres and

knew our traditional English pantomime, upon both of which the ballet was based, I did not enjoy it. It was too muddled, although I laughed at Lifar's dance as the Sailor. It was so unlike any hornpipe I had ever seen.

Balanchine's next ballet was *La Chatte* (1927) based on Aesop's fable of the cat and the mouse. On stage was set a huge mouse-trap made of transparent talc (something like today's Perspex) against a background of shiny black American cloth. The dancers too were dressed in these extraordinary materials. All was undoubtedly very up-to-date, but it did not please me. I had gone specially to see Alicia Markova dance the cat, for my fellow student was now a ballerina, but the glittering bits on her costume and the reflection of light from the shiny surfaces spoilt the lines of her beautiful dancing.

Balanchine's most important ballets for Diaghilev were *Apollon Musagetes* (now known as *Apollo*) and *The Prodigal Son* (1929). They are still danced by several companies and are very different. *Apollo* tells you how the newly born god is taught by the Muses of Dance (Terpsichore), Epic Poetry (Calliope) and Mime (Polymnia) and is a wonderful demonstration of Balanchine's co-operation with Stravinsky's music. Like *The Prodigal Son*, *Apollo* was created to display the talents of Serge Lifar. When Nijinska rejoined Diaghilev in 1923 she brought this young student with her from Kiev. He was not then ready to appear, so was set to work with Nicholas Legat, specially brought to Monte Carlo to train both Lifar and Danilova. By hard work Lifar soon became a principal dancer and Diaghilev also felt he had the makings of a choreographer. This career in fact began later when Lifar went to the Paris Opera after Diaghilev's death.

Lifar with Nikitina, Tchernicheva and Doubrovska in *Apollo*

The Prodigal Son. 'Never darken my doors again' and 'The Return'. (New York City Ballet)

Diaghilev had always wanted to present a story from the bible. *The Legend of Joseph*, when he brought Massine to his company was only one attempt. For *The Prodigal Son* he brought together three artists who understood that great sincerity was wanted for such a ballet and they felt the subject deeply. Balanchine, the choreographer, might have been a priest; Prokofiev, the Russian composer, often concealed his deep love of classical church music by daring attempts to make modern sounds; whilst Georges Roualt was the French artist noted for his tragic paintings of Christ in Agony. These three men told the old story of *The Prodigal Son* very simply and dramatically and although the movements sometimes seemed ugly and jerky, I was not the only person to weep when the Son at last crawled to the gate and was picked up by his father and carried home.

Sadly enough *The Prodigal Son*, with its success and promise of serious work to come, was Diaghilev's last ballet. He died in Venice shortly after, mourned by the world of ballet lovers. For twenty years his company had dominated ballet, forming the tastes of many people – your grand-parents, your parents and you too, because many of his ballets are still favourites everywhere. Perhaps they do not seem quite so wonderful to you now. Other choreographers, composers, artists and dancers have learnt from Diaghilev's example and when his company broke up after his death it was by no means the end of his work. In the ten years between his death in 1929 and the outbreak of the 1939–45 War, his choreographers and dancers travelled everywhere. They settled in many different countries taking his ballets and teachings with them. It is interesting to make a list of them.

Those coming to London to teach, open schools and sometimes start companies were: Seraphina Astafieva (1912) amongst whose pupils were Anton Dolin and Dames Alicia Markova and Margot Fonteyn; Mikhail Mordkin who danced with Pavlova in 1910 and then taught in England before going to America; Serge Morosoff who taught Ruth French; Tamara Karsavina (1917) whose work in England needs a book on its own; Dame Marie Rambert (1919) without whose enthusiasm English ballet might never have started and who first taught the beginnings of choreography to Sir Frederick Ashton, Anthony Tudor and later Norman Morrice and many others: Lydia Kyasht (1920) who first came here to take over the ballerina rôle from Dame Adeline Genée in 1908; Laurent Novikoff (1928), who danced with Anna Pavlova; and finally Nicholas Legat (1937) who joined Diaghilev as teacher when Maestro Cecchetti settled in London to teach.

Diaghilev's choreographers similarly travelled everywhere before settling permanently and here is a brief list of what they did.

Mikhail Fokine returned to Russia in 1912 and worked in many European countries before settling in America in 1918. But he frequently returned to Europe to stage old and make new ballets for different companies including some for our English dancer, Ruth French.

Leonide Massine left Diaghilev in 1920 to work in London and other European cities, returning to the Russian ballet in 1925 before going to America in 1927. Since then he has been welcomed in every continent, staging old and new ballets and working upon his system of notation, which may well prove to be one way of teaching young choregraphers more about movement and how to use it.

Bronislava Nijinska left Diaghilev to join Ida Rubinstein, then worked in many European countries before finally settling in America. Georges Balanchine left Europe in 1933 to help Lincoln Kerstein found the American School of Ballet from which was ultimately created the New York City Ballet, now the foremost American Company.

Serge Lifar became principal dancer at the Paris Opera immediately after Diaghilev's death and by 1932 had been promoted Professor of Dance. He was thus able to re-organise both the training and repertoire of this oldest of classical schools of dance and reinstate it as one of the leading companies in the world.

Russian Ballet after Diaghilev

Diaghilev's dancers and choreographers were not the only members of the Maryinsky and Bolshoi ballets to leave Russia. The Revolution caused many others to emigrate to find work. Four of the ballerinas, Mathilde Kesshinskaya, Olga Preobrazhenskaya, Lubov Egorova and Vera Trefilova started schools in Paris. Others went to Europe, South Africa, Australia and the Americas. Students from such schools then joined the various Russian ballet companies which were formed and re-formed in the period between Diaghilev's death and the 1939–45 War.

It was from Preobrazhenskaya's school that Baronova, Riaboushinska and Toumanova, the so-called 'baby ballerinas', with David Lichine, a pupil of Egorova and Nijinska, came to join Ballets Russes de Monte Carlo. This first attempt to re-start the Diaghilev company was made by René Blum, director of the Monte Carlo Opera who invited the dancers to appear in the operas and persuaded Balanchine to create two ballets specially for this new company. These were La Concurrence and Cotillon (1932). The former told of two tailors quarrelling in the street outside their shops in order to attract customers! Cotillon was a charming set of dances at a ball. Both were very successful and showed Balanchine's mastery of movement even in comparison with the older ballets of Massine and Fokine, danced by older Diaghilev stars such as Lubov Tchernicheva, Leon Woizikovsky and Alexandra Danilova. These older ballets were staged by Serge Grigoriev, perhaps the most important member of Diaghilev's company. His name is too little known and the job he did too little understood. This is a pity, for today's ballet world could learn much from his example.

Serge Grigoriev graduated from the Imperial St. Petersburg School as a mime and character dancer. As a student his marvellous memory attracted the attention of Fokine who welcomed him as a colleague when Diaghilev invited Grigoriev to join his first Paris season as régisseur which, translated roughly, means stage-manager. But in Russia it means much more and Grigoriev possibly made it the most important job in Diaghilev's company. Although he played many character rôles, he also rehearsed the company in every part of the repertoire. He knew exactly what costumes, wigs and make-up everyone had to wear and how they should be worn. He would set up the stage with scenery, props and lighting. He would correct the conductor and musicians and, if necessary conduct their playing and singing when it took place behind scenes. He organised such things as the complicated baggage and travelling arrangements. Yet he always remained cool and in complete control. I well remember meeting him and dear Lubov Tchernicheva, his wife, at a Golders Green grocer's where they were making up their minds which tea and biscuits I would like, for I was on my way to visit them. His greeting and invitation to make my own choice reminded me of his lovely gesture as the Russian Father in La Boutique Fantasque, when he set down his little girl and opened his arms as if to say: 'Please, there is the whole shop to choose from!' This, then, was the man who, helped by his great dancer wife, was continually reconstructing the Diaghilev ballets for one company or another.

The first attempt to reform Diaghilev's company and preserve some of his great ballets, as well as create new ones for both young and older dancers, led to violent quarrels, both complicated and sad because they only led to one company after another fighting for and then losing their stars and their ballets. We hope by now all is forgiven and forgotten, for such quarrels should play no part in our history. What is more important is to tell you about Massine's new type of ballet.

The Symphonic Ballet

When Balanchine went to America in 1933, Massine became chief choreographer for Colonel De Basil's Ballets Russes de Monte Carlo, the 'baby ballerinas' and David Lichine playing a very important part in his new Symphonic Ballets. In the absence of a Diaghilev always looking for composers willing to create serious ballet music, Massine turned to the great classical composers and made his first attempts to interpret a symphony. This was Les Présages (or Fate) in 1933 danced to Tchaikovsky's Fifth Symphony.

Its theme was borrowed from the composer's own thoughts about Man struggling against Fate. Behind each movement lay the idea that if Man (danced by David Lichine) had: 1. Action; 2. Love; 3. Fun and happiness, then in the 4th and final movement he would triumph. Most ballet lovers and many musicians found this an exciting work, though some music lovers were horrified. But sitting high in the amphitheatre of the Opera House, I got very excited with the first movement. Somehow the Girl representing Action (Verchinina) helped me to see how much energy, discipline and sheer love of work had to be put into dancing if it were to carry meaning. The second movement made me happy yet sad at the same time because the two Young Lovers (Baronova and Lichine) were

61

constantly being torn apart by the strange bat-like figure representing Fate. The light, gay dancing (Riabouchinska and *corps de ballet*) in the third movement was joyous and when in the last movement the three leading dancers helped Man to drive Fate from the stage, I was thrilled. Massine's choreography had shown me that classical dance could have quite another value. It could make you think very deeply and not just tell stories.

Massine's *Choréatium* danced to Brahms' Fourth Symphony showed another way to interpret classical music and a way which many other choreographers used later. Ernest Newman, one of England's greatest music critics loved this ballet and wrote: 'The ballet works itself out consistently as a design, reproducing in the subtlest way the design of the music . . . . The more musical we are and the better we know our Brahms, the more pleasure we derive from *Choréatium*'. I know I learnt more about the music than ever before and when I went to a concert soon after with another famous critic and friend, Edwin Evans. He did not say as he usually did – 'Have you read the score? I want you to listen for –'. Instead he merely said: 'Remember what *Choréatium* said to you'. And this was what my eight-year-old nephew said to me after watching *Symphonic Variations* in 1946, Sir Frederick Ashton's great masterpiece in classical dance: 'I know all about the music now, the dancers told me.'

Massine's Third Symphonic ballet was to Berlioz's *Symphonie Fantastique*. It interpreted the composer's own story, so few people argued about its success. But Massine's interpretation of Beethoven's Seventh Symphony was a failure. He tried to tell stories from the Bible as well as stories of the gods of Olympus, and none of them fitted the music. This lesson is one which some later choreographers have still not learnt; they try to put stories to music which already has some meaning of its own, and find the two just will not fit.

In England

The death of Diaghilev, shortly followed by that of Anna Pavlova, put an end to any hopes English dancers had of joining either of their companies. Although *ballets d'action* had first been produced in London and Weaver's ideas had triumphed on the continent, no attempt had been made to start an English ballet. There was plenty of work for an English *corps de ballet* and second soloists without one because theatre managers had imported the greatest international stars and ballets from abroad to entertain their English audiences, from the time of Le Grand Dupré and Marie Sallé to Adeline Genée and Lydia Kyasht. The last two had starred in the Alhambra and Empire Ballets from 1897 and it was only after Kyasht returned to Russia in 1914 that Phyllis Bedells became the first English prima ballerina. But Diaghilev's new works had made the ballets in which she appeared seem old-fashioned so despite her charm and lively dancing, the Empire Ballet had to close down in 1917.

A Beginning

But English ballet began to rise to fame slowly but steadily. It began when Marie Rambert opened her school in 1919. She had joined Diaghilev originally to help Nijinsky with the music of *The Rite of Spring* and then worked with his company studying under Maestro Cecchetti until she met and married Ashley Dukes, an English author and critic. The dancers she trained were first introduced to audiences in plays and revues, and at that time they were known as the Rambert Dancers. But in 1930 she founded the Ballet Club at the Mercury Theatre in Notting Hill Gate. You could go there on Sunday evenings and watch excerpts from famous ballets and, more excitingly, new works from young choreographers trying out ideas under Marie Rambert's guidance. It soon became evident that in Frederick Ashton she had a choreographer of great promise. Under the name of the Rambert Ballet she sometimes gave short London Theatre seasons in which Alicia Markova and Tamara Karsavina both danced. Her dancers also took part in the Sunday evening performances of the Camargo Society, another thread in the history of English Ballet.

The Camargo Society

In 1929 three ballet lovers, Philip Richardson, editor of *The Dancing Times*, Edwin Evans, music critic and Arnold Haskell, author and later director of the Royal Ballet Schools, met to discuss how they could encourage English artists who had danced, composed and designed for Diaghilev and other companies. They invited many of these artists as well as leading teachers to attend a dinner party at which the Camargo Society was born, with the aim of presenting English ballet. After the financial problems had been solved, usually through the generosity of friends and the expert advice of Maynard Keynes, Lydia Lopokova's husband, the Society's Sunday evening performances began. They quickly showed how much talent was waiting to be used, particularly from the Rambert and Vic-Wells ballets. These dancers often joined forces to appear in older items but most important were the ballets created by their own choreographers. Foremost among these was Frederick Ashton with *Capriol Suite* in 1930, *Façade* in 1931 and others, together with Ninette de Valois, whose *Job, A Masque for Dancing* in 1931 was the Society's greatest success.

Diaghilev had originally commissioned this score from Vaughan Williams, but rejected it as being 'too English'. However, it was its very Englishness that made it so marvellous to watch. The choregraphy is based on *The Book of Job* illustrated by William Blake. 'It tells how Satan tempts Job, who curses the day he was born and sees Satan sitting on God's throne to send down War, Pestilence and Famine. But Elihu, who is young and beautiful teaches Job to look up and hope. Job sees Satan thrown down from Heaven and God returned to his throne. He can again sit in

Above and top right: Anton Dolin as Satan and Job with his comforters in *Job*

Centre: Margot Fonteyn and **bottom:** Robert Helpmann in early appearances for the Sadlers' Wells Ballet

peace surrounded by his family.' The solemn beauty of the English church and court music upon which Vaughan Williams built his score, and the simple way the old bible story was told by Blake's imaginative drawings, inspired Ninette de Valois to create an unusual dance style for that time. Her dancers were barefoot and used no turn-out. Their movements flowed from one picture to another as the various characters moved into and out of the fascinating pictures drawn by Blake. She made a striking difference between the dancing of the good and evil characters, particularly in the dances for Satan (Anton Dolin). The awful strength and evil Satan showed when he temped Job made many of us realise that in Ninette de Valois English ballet had found a fearless personality able to strike out on her own without neglecting the English traditions which have made our theatre so unique. She once said, when talking about the use of classical technique: 'You must have rules in order to break them if you wish to give your choreography greater meaning.'

The Camargo Society's performances aroused so much interest that in 1932 it gave a season at the Savoy Theatre. Its repertoire consisted of some sixteen ballets in which appeared many important dancers whose work was playing

The Lord of Burleigh, one of Ashton's first ballets for the Sadlers' Wells with Leslie Edwards, Richard Ellis and Pearl Argyle

Dame Ninette de Valois in *Barabau*

and continues to play an important part in English ballet. Amongst the names can be found Ninette de Valois, Alicia Markova, Lydia Lopokova, Phyllis Bedells, Ruth French, Urusula Moreton, Frederick Ashton, William Chappell and Walter Gore. The orchestra was conducted by no less a genius than Sir Thomas Beecham (the first to bring Diaghilev to London) and also by Constant Lambert, whose wisdom and brilliant handling of choreographers, music, orchestras and dancers helped to make the Royal Ballet into one of the finest in the world. But the real success of the season was *Giselle* danced by the ballerina Olga Spessitseva with Anton Dolin as her Albrecht. The Camargo Society proved that London at least, was ready for English ballet.

By 1933 the Camargo Society decided it had fulfilled its aim. As a closing effort Maynard Keynes organised two Gala performances for the Government Hospitality Fund in honour of the World Economic Conference. Queen Mary and other members of the Royal Family attended the first Gala and the Opera House was packed on both occasions so, after paying its debts and expenses, what money was left the Society gave to the now well-established Vic-Wells ballet. Its ballets were divided between that company and the Rambert Ballet now working regularly in its own home, the Mercury Theatre.

Ninette de Valois

Ninette de Valois was not only a choreographer. After a varied career as a solo dancer in music halls, pantomimes and operas, she joined Diaghilev for a short time, but decided his type of new ballet for the sake of being new did not always suit her taste. She felt she must branch out and start a company to create ballets in keeping with her own ideas. To do this she realised she must have dancers able to respond to her wishes and so she opened her own school in 1926. She found work for her students at the Abbey Theatre, Dublin where they performed in *Plays for Dancers*, specially written by the Irish poet, W. B. Yeats; at the Arts Theatre, Cambridge as the Chorus in Greek Plays and, most important, in the operas and Shakespeare plays produced at the Old Vic.

This battered old theatre, once a music hall, became the birthplace of the National Theatre, the English National Opera and the Royal Ballet; and its audiences grew until a second theatre had to be built to house the Sadlers' Wells Opera and Ballet. All this happened through the efforts of its owner, 'The Lady' as everyone called the strangely forbidding yet homely Dame Lilian Baylis. Dame Lilian believed only the best was good enough for her audiences, who were mainly drawn from unfashionable parts of London, and it was those audiences who helped to build the reputation of the ballet thanks to Ninette de Valois, who was not content merely to train dancers and work as their choreographer. She also taught the audience about the difficulties of classical technique and ballet-making and, through her dancers, she made people understand the sheer joy of dance. She also made them think, for if she

L'Après-midi d'un Faune: Bakst's original design for the
Faun, danced by Nijinsky

Rex Whistler's designs for *The Rake's Progress*

sometimes presented ballets which were full of dance like her own *Les Petits Riens* and *Fête Polonaise* and Ashton's *Les Rendezvous* and *Les Patineurs*, she also gave them very serious works like her own *Job*, *The Rake's Progress* and *Checkmate* and Ashton's haunting *Apparitions*, delicate *Nocturne* and tragic *Dante Sonata*.

Progress Report

If you look at any ballet book published between 1930–39 you will think that the Russian companies were the most important. This is not so. Please remember that during those nine years the various Russian companies visited London only during the Season, that is May and June and during that time they occupied the main London Theatres. The Rambert and Sadlers' Wells Ballets appeared in these theatres only briefly, after the foreign companies had gone, but they danced regularly in their own theatres once or twice a week throughout the year. Those of us who believed in English Ballet could therefore enjoy it more or less all the time. The others, who only saved up for the annual feast of Russian Ballet, did not know what they missed. They were people who believed that 'No English can dance'. But Marie Rambert and Ninette de Valois were laying the solid foundations of English Ballet. Their methods were different, but between them they guided English choreographers and dancers to the top. Today instead of companies and schools all over the world being led by Russians, as they were in the 'thirties, it is very often choreographers, teachers and dancers who were either born in England or came here to learn their job, who lead these companies.

Marie Rambert's most important work was to encourage and guide choreographers. Her experiences with Diaghilev had taught her they must rely on dance alone to convey through simple movements the moods, emotions and actions of the characters in their ballets. She could not spend money as he had done on expensive sets and costumes, although she sometimes managed to commission special music. Moreover the styles of dance used had to be suitable for her young dancers, whose technique was not as expert as that of Alicia Markova who often appeared with them. Ninette de Valois, although using young choreographers, believed she must first concentrate on her students' technique if they were to perform in the ballets she hoped to produce when they and her choreographers had had more experience. This was why the Sadlers' Wells repertoire contained such important ballets as *Coppélia*, *Carnaval*, *Les Sylphides*, *Swan-Lake* and *The Nutcracker*. Most of these starred Alicia Markova sometimes partnered by Stanislas Idzikovsky, both of whom set an extremely high standard for the rest of the cast to follow. *Giselle* was the last revival staged specially for Alicia Markova, with Anton Dolin as her Albrecht. It was possibly the most important event for these two famous English dancers. It marked the beginning of a partnership which brought pleasure to many people in many places. Sadly it also broke

The Rake's Progress. **Top**: the Orgy and **above**: Harold Turner as the Rake

the ties that had existed between them and the Sadlers' Wells ballet since the opening of its theatre in 1931. In 1935 they left to form their own company – the Markova-Dolin Ballet which later became London's Festival Ballet. But before leaving Alicia Markova danced in one of the most important ballets in the company's history, *The Rake's Progress*, a truly English ballet with choreography by Ninette de Valois.

A young singer-musician, Gavin Gordon, had been inspired by the paintings of *The Rake's Progress* by William Hogarth, which hang in the Sir John Soane Museum in Lincoln's Inn Fields. The ballet 'tells of an 18th century Young Man, the Rake, who inherits vast wealth but squanders it all on wine, women and gambling and dies in the mad-house.' Hogarth painted several such series in his efforts to make Londoners understand the evils of wealth and poverty of his day. Anybody who studies *The Rake's*

Progress, particularly after seeing the ballet, will understand how Ninette de Valois has brought those pictures to life. She has not used all of them, only those which show firstly; 'how the Rake is surrounded by jockey, friend, gambler, teachers of fencing, music and dancing, tailor and wig-maker all trying to take his money, when in comes the Young Girl he has betrayed. Then you see him surrounded by blowsy women singing, dancing and drinking until he is so drunk that he throws his money everywhere. His creditors come after him, but his debts are paid by the Young Girl, who still loves him. But this does not stop his follies. He gambles and loses all. As he plays his last card, it is trumped. He goes mad. The final scene is in the madhouse where fashionable ladies have come to gaze at the tragic inmates. The Young Girl too comes to find the Rake. But he does not recognise her nor understand her tender caress until he suddenly rises to give her the kiss she has hoped for, and falls dead at her feet.'

The Rake's Progress held and still holds its audience by Ninette de Valois' brilliant choreography, by Gavin Gordon's interesting music based on old London Street Songs and Ballads and by Rex Whistler's scenery and costumes which capture the colour, period and feeling of Hogarth's drawings. It also shows its audience that it is not enough for a dancer to rely on technique. In ballets like *The Rake's Progress* you must live your part and allow the choreographer to discipline your movements, fitting them into the pictures about the lives of people in other times and other places. Moreover it is important to dance as you are directed when the pictures you are helping to bring to life are as well-known as those in Blake's *Book of Job* and Hogarth's *The Rake's Progress.* So, by 1935, Ninette de Valois had proved her dancers were capable of meeting the technical demands of *Swan-Lake* and *Giselle* and were also developing into artists of high rank able to work in new forms of ballet. Although she always believed that classical technique was the firm base on which to build, she recognised that away from the classroom its rules can be broken and very different styles of dance developed.

You could call *Job* a ballet in modern barefoot style based on movements which flow in rounded lines for all the good characters, but which become angular and jerky when danced by the evil ones. Ninette de Valois worked this style out for herself, just as Nijinsky worked out one for his *L'Aprés-Midi d'un Faune;* in neither case did the choreographers use it for any other ballet. You can call *The Rake's Progress* a *demi-character* ballet, whose style is dictated by Hogarth's pictures. If you contrast the Dancing Master's solo with those of the rest of the characters you will more easily understand what I mean. He follows all the rules of the classroom, the rest of the characters frequently break them.

Ninette de Valois created another style based on classical technique when she created *The Haunted Ballroom* (1934) specially to show the unusual talent of Robert Helpmann. He had joined the company from Australia in 1933 and first danced in the *corps de ballet* of *Coppélia.* He was the actor-dancer who meant so much to the company from the moment he joined to the time when he finally left in 1950. His first major rôle was in *The Haunted Ballroom* based on a story by Edgar Allan Poe. 'The Master of Treginnis is persuaded by his three lady guests to show them the haunted ballroom where he reluctantly allows them to dance before saying Good-night. He returns there at midnight when ghosts from the past force him to dance to death. In the morning his son finds his dead body and realises he too will meet the same fate'. The plot is a little like that of *Giselle* – that is, partly in the earthly world of ordinary people and partly about the world of ghosts or dreams. It demanded a romantic style which Ninette de Valois created for the guests with softly rounded arms and delicate *pointe-work*, which is at the same time elegant and fashionable. But for her ghosts she used a freer form of dance to give the effect that these ghostly shapes move faster and faster encircling and buffeting the tragic Master until he dies, exhausted.

The success of these two ballets did not prevent Ninette de Valois realising that she could not take all the responsibility for creating new ballets and organising her companies' repertoire. She now had to concentrate on the training of those dancers who would have to take over all the major rôles now that Alicia Markova was leaving. She therefore invited Frederick Ashton to join the Sadlers' Wells Ballet as chief choreographer. They were already dancing some of his ballets and by 1935 he had shown the wide range of styles that he still continues to use, from the truly comic to the most tragic, and including his few ballets which show only the purity of the English classical school of dance.

Sir Frederick Ashton (b. 1904)

Frederick Ashton did not start dancing very young, but such was the impression made on him by Anna Pavlova that he finally began to study under Massine and then Marie Rambert. She quickly realised his unique choreographic talent and set him to work staging a ballet suitable for her dancers who were about to appear in a revue at the Lyric Theatre, Hammersmith. *A Tragedy of Fashion* (1926) may only have been a frivolous item in a gay revue for fashionable audiences. But it made an impression on serious ballet-lovers because of its original movements. It started Ashton on his search for knowledge which he began by joining the Ida Rubinstein company in Paris to work under Massine and Nijinska. To the latter he owed much of his insight into choreographic problems, the use of movement and its vocabulary and the relationship between music and dance which he had began to study with Marie Rambert. He returned to London to stage the first of the ballets – over eighty of them – which he has created since 1926.

From the beginning of his career Ashton's work has always shown some distinguishing marks. His trade-marks we might call them because they are always evident in his ballets. I always remember *Capriol Suite* when it was staged

Sir Frederick Ashton in *Nocturne*

for the first Rambert Ballet season in 1930. It was danced to Peter Warlock's arrangement of some Elizabethan dances found in the Fitzwilliam Virginal Book. In it Ashton showed his love of and belief in English traditions by using movements from court, folk and Morris dances. He also showed the gaily comic and serious sides of his nature. Two dances, *Mattachins* and *Pieds en l'Air* were later developed in *La Fille Mal Gardée* into Alain's solo when he hilariously mimics classical dance and the boys' stick dance. But the sad *Pavane* introduced us to Ashton's exquisite use of *ports de bras* when telling a story. 'In it Two Youths offer, one a rose, the other a poem to a beautiful girl because they love her. But she rejects them firmly and sadly.'

It is impossible to describe all Ashton's ballets – they need a book of their own. And it is equally impossible to overestimate what he means to us in English ballet today. History shows there are two kinds of choreographer. The first create ballets because they must, feeling there is no other way to tell the story or idea which has inspired them and which they feel they can interpret only by some special form of dance. The second are those who create a ballet round the special talent and qualities of a particular dancer or group of dancers, and feel they must display these gifts to the best advantage. Both choreographers are of the utmost value. The first often change history because they

enlarge their dancers' and their audience's knowledge of movement, making them all think more deeply about the characters played. This is what Fokine did when staging *The Firebird*, *Petrushka* and other ballets with Tamara Karsavina and Nijinsky, Massine with many dancers and Ninette de Valois for her company in *Job* and *The Rake's Progress*. The other kind of choreographer displays the natural, often unique, talents of his dancer in such a way that he makes a star. This is what Filipo Taglioni did for his daughter, Marie, Perrot for Carlotta Grisi and Frederick Ashton for Margot Fonteyn.

When Ashton joined Sadlers' Wells he began to develop Margot Fonteyn's unusual talents. She had already appeared in some minor rôles but her first solo part was in Ninette de Valois' *The Haunted Ballroom*, where her dramatic gesture as the Young Master of Treginnis when he finds his father dead, made us all catch our breath. It was so full of dread, so tragic yet so beautiful. This then was the star for whom Ashton was to create his greatest ballets. The first important one was *Apparitions* in 1936 whose story you have already read. It was the most expensive production the company had yet staged and this was due to the wonderful generosity of Constant Lambert, who thought out the plot, chose music by Liszt, but gave his fees to Gordon Jacob for the orchestration and secondly to Cecil Beaton, who designed costumes and scenery. The latter was improvised from white flats and draperies so lit that they cast strange shadows and made the colour of the costumes extremely important. The set also emphasised the beauty of the ballroom costumes made by the most famous of ballet costumiers, Madame Karinska to whom Beaton paid his fee. But it was the beautiful dancing of Margot Fonteyn as the Woman in the Ball-gown and her understanding of this rôle, together with the passionate mime of Robert Helpmann as the Poet that made this ballet such a success.

In the same year, shortly after *Apparitions*, Ashton staged a most delicate work. *Nocturne* was a brief and tragic episode. 'A simple flower-girl falls in love with a Rich Young Man. He loves her for a moment, but leaves her when his Rich Beauty returns, leaving the Flower-girl heartbroken. The elderly Spectator fails to console her and he walks sadly away to watch the dawn break over the great city of Paris'. Those of us who saw Ashton play this tiny part will never forget his gestures. He laid his hand on the Young Girl's shoulder, but realising he could do nothing, let it drop and turned to walk up the steps of a balcony. There he raised his arms to welcome the dawn, but let them drop helplessly. How simple it sounds. Yet even today you would understand that for all the Spectator's sympathy – he was only an outsider at this tragedy and – could do nothing.

It was in *Nocturne*, too, that Ashton made us realise how many ways he could use an *arabesque* to convey meaning. This is perhaps the most important feature of his choreography. Very rarely does he use steps as you dance them in the class-room. There is some detail in the *ports de bras*, the angle or level of the leg, the turn or twist of the body and above all in the way he joins steps together that makes them look different. It was this continual adjustment of her movements to his choreography that turned Margot Fonteyn into the greatest Aurora of *The Sleeping Beauty*.

Top: *Horoscope*, Sir Frederick Ashton's first ballet for Margot Fonteyn and Michael Somes

Centre: *Façade*

Above: *A Wedding Bouquet*, with Dame Ninette as Webster

As Aurora she had, of course, to rely on the rules of classical dance which she had practised and mastered in the classroom every working day since she began dancing. But instead of having always to concentrate on the changes in the movements she had to dance to express the moods, emotions and actions of the characters Ashton created for her, she was able to relax and enjoy herself as a Princess should on her birthday, when dreaming of her Prince and then at her wedding.

The Ashton ballets described so far all tell a story. There were others which only had a theme like *Les Rendezvous* (or Lovers' Meetings) in 1933, which was made for the Sadlers' Wells ballet and danced by Alicia Markova and Stanislas Idzikovsky. Another favourite was – and is – *Les Patineurs* staged in 1937 to display the brilliant dancing of Harold Turner as the Blue Boy. It immediately made him into a star for whom Ninette de Valois created a magnificent solo as the Red Knight in her *Checkmate*. In *Les Patineurs* there are both Blue Boys and Blue Girls. They represent the truly professional skaters who can do all the virtuoso steps. On the first night Harold Turner, Mary Honer and Elizabeth Miller dazzled us with their turns and *pirouettes*, so you can imagine how excited we were to see English dancers spinning like some of the Russians we knew. It was in the same ballet that one of the *corps de ballet* astounded us with his elevation. This was Michael Somes who became Margot Fonteyn's partner for the first time in *Horoscope* in 1938 – the beginning of a partnership for whom Ashton created his most important ballets when the company was firmly established at the Royal Opera House after the war.

In *Horoscope* we saw for the first time the sympathetic relationship between these two young dancers that made their interpretation of many different rôles so wonderful to watch. They were intensely musical and had the same feeling for line, and if their mimed dance was not so dramatically intense as it became in later ballets like *Ondine* in 1958, their timing, phrasing and the sincerity of their movements made us all believe in this tale of two lovers born under different signs of the Zodiac being brought together first by the Gemini and then by the Moon. Both the libretto and the music were by Constant Lambert, that marvellous musician who had dedicated his life to the well-being of the Sadlers' Wells Ballet. The costumes and sets were yet another example of Sophie Fedorovitch's uncanny feeling for the need to disclose and never hide the movements. They were simple and revealed the lines of dance whilst creating the right atmosphere for a ballet dealing with the fate of two young people.

But Ashton was not always gaily comic or seriously dramatic. He could also be sophisticated and frivolous. One of his first efforts in this manner had been *Façade*, staged for the Camargo Society in 1931. It still makes us laugh, particularly those of us who remember the types of dance at which he is poking fun, including classical ballet. I shall never forget the inelegant way Ashton himself upset Lydia Lopokova's dignity when – in the Tango – he turned her over his arm with her legs straight and her feet unpointed. I laughed as much if not more when Helpmann did exactly the same with Margot Fonteyn when the ballet was staged for Sadlers' Wells. Another frivolous ballet was *A Wedding Bouquet* in 1937 danced to words by Gertrude Stein with music, set and costumes by Lord Berners. It could have been called: 'How not to behave at a wedding', so many awkward people came. Josephine who 'should not go to a wedding' gets drunk; Violet chases a nervous Ernest; Forlorn Julia keeps getting between the Bride and her Groom; and Pepe, the little dog is very troublesome. On the company's twenty-first birthday many of the original cast returned to play their parts. The biggest applause was for Ninette de Valois as the fussy maid, 'Webster, a name that was spoken', and Constant Lambert, toasting his colleagues in champagne as he spoke the words. But many things had happened before this twenty-first birthday party.

The Rambert Ballet

Frederick Ashton's departure from the Rambert Ballet by no means put a stop to its activities. On the contrary Rambert was already encouraging other choregraphers. Although the work of the two most important of them, Andrée Howard and Antony Tudor is not so well known as it should be, they both made valuable contributions to the repertoire. Fête Etrange, Lilac Garden and Dark Elegies all add to the understanding of other ideas of using movement.

Andrée Howard was a dancer and choreographer who sometimes designed her own scenery and costumes. Thus her ballets always told you a great deal about her sensitive feelings for those movements which describe moods rather than great dramas. Her first ballet, in 1933, was Our Lady's Juggler, based on a medieval legend. 'An old Juggler is ending his life in a monastery and realising he has no gift to bring to His Lady, decides to give her the only thing he knows. At midnight he goes to the chapel in his juggler's clothes to dance and juggle before the statue of Our Lady. The abbot, hearing a noise comes down, but is amazed to see that Our Lady comes down from her pedestal to comfort and bless the old man when he falls exhausted.' The ballet showed Andrée Howard's originality. She created interesting movements from one of Breughel's pictures of peasants dancing, as well as borrowing poses copied from the Commedia dell'Arte players. Andrée Howard's next important work, in 1939, was, like many of her ballets, based on a novel, David Garnett's Lady Into Fox tells of a girl who changes into a fox and is then hunted by those who had been her neighbours. Such a ballet had never been seen before and the brilliant way Andrée Howard introduces fox-like movements into the Girl's dance before she is transformed, makes one understand this strange character. Much later on the French choreographer, Roland Petit, used similar animal movements; cat movements when he created Les Demoiselles de la Nuit about a man falling in love with a cat (danced by Margot Fonteyn) and wolf-like movement in Le Loup about a young girl who falls in love with a wolf.

Andrée Howard's Fête Etrange was inspired by an episode in a novel by the Frenchman, Fournier. 'A country boy wanders into the grounds of a chateau, where he meets its young mistress, who is about to be married. Shyly he joins in the dances at the betrothal party, but without

understanding his feelings for this young girl and hers for him, he destroys the relationship between this gentle girl and her fiancé. Sadly each one leaves the garden, alone.' Danced to music and song by Fauré, this is one of the most delicate of all ballets. So little is said, it is only felt. The dancers playing the three leading rôles express moods and hide their deep emotions whilst the corps de ballet, although they catch these moods, are only onlookers to set the time and place of the story. The ballet is also notable for the exquisite colouring and delicacy of Sophie Fedorovitch's set and costumes. The soft drapery hanging above a flight of stairs conjures up the spacious chateau grounds seen beyond the balcony when the evenings draw in and frost sparkles on the leaves. This masterpiece was created for the newly formed London Ballet which danced at Toynbee Hall and elsewhere until after war broke out. It then amalgamated with the Rambert Ballet from which most of its dancers and many of its ballets had come.

Antony Tudor came late to dancing but, like Ashton, quickly showed his choreographic talent and by 1931 was already at work. Both he and Ashton had several things in common at this period, notably the way they related their dance to the music under the keen eyes of Marie Rambert. But whereas Ashton's movements involved every part of the dancer's body to give it expression, Tudor's movements relied more on some tiny detail in the arm, hand or head. In other words, Ashton tried to help both dancers and audience to understand clearly and simply what emotions made each movement necessary, whilst Tudor preferred his dancers and audience to keep their deeper feelings hidden. This was certainly evident in Lilac Garden in 1936. Danced to music by Chausson it tells how 'a betrothed couple each meet a lover from their past. The Bride-to-be steals some passionate moments with her lover. But the man she must marry stiffly rejects the young woman in his past despite her emotional pleading. Such intimate scenes are interrupted by friends who deplore such unconventional behaviour.' The old relationships are therefore only superficially explored by the Betrothed Couple, who eventually take arms and walk stiffly away together. The strains of these intimate meetings are best seen in a small theatre, for Tudor prefers his dancers to use little or no facial expression but rely on tiny movements which describe their frustration at not being able to express openly their innermost feelings.

Dark Elegies, Tudor's next major work in 1937, was most unusual. The music came from Mahler's Songs on the Death of Children, the composer's attempt to give musical expression to Rückert's poems which described the feelings of simple peasants and fisherfolk on the death of a child. Mahler caught the tragic despair and sentiment behind the words, but Tudor did not attempt to interpret them. Instead he tried to convey the emotions of simple folk, to whom words mean little, by using movement which today we should call 'modern dance'. But unlike today's modern dancers who spend much time on floor-work and often dance as individuals, Tudor's dancers were a group, all feeling the same sorrow and despair, and when first one and then another danced alone it was because at that moment his or her grief became unbearable and had to be expressed more fully than in the simple circle and chain dances of the group. This ballet was one of the first times an English choreographer used a song cycle as inspiration. It has been done several times since then. For example Walter Gore interpreted the words of two poems by Robert Browning, *Porphyria's Lover* and *Confessional*, and allowed both their meaning and rhythm to dictate the shape and phrasing of the steps and gestures of the dance instead of using music. Kenneth MacMillan later interpreted Mahler's *Song of the Earth* in somewhat the same way. But in every case, particularly in the two works by Mahler, it is not really necessary to understand the words. The quality and expression in the dancers' movements should explain the moods and emotions of the poems.

Tudor left Rambert after the success of *Dark Elegies* to form his own London Ballet, leaving Walter Gore and Frank Staff as choreographers. Shortly after war broke out he left for America and has worked there ever since, returning only to revive old ballets and to create *Shadow Play* for the Royal Ballet. But this has little of the sensitivity of his early works and nothing of the impact of his masterpiece, *Pillar of Fire* which he made for American Ballet Theatre and was the great dramatic success when this company first visited London after the war.

Although in 1937 Marie Rambert lost Tudor as well as some important dancers, she had Walter Gore and Frank Staff to provide interesting ballets for her company. The dancers often required great acting ability for such rôles as *Lady Into Fox* and Walter Gore's danced poems. Amongst the talented interpreters were Sally Gilmour and Celia Franca, as well as the two choreographers themselves. The company began to tour and give flying matinées in provincial towns, where, sometimes, English ballet was seen for the first time. Provincial tours were also undertaken by Dance Theatre, directed by Antony Tudor and the American dancer-choreographer, Agnes de Mille. Thus by the summer of 1939 there existed three English companies offering a wide choice of ballets from the great classics to the most modern of their day.

The War Clouds Gather

By 1937 English Ballet had truly found a place in the theatre and for the next two years began to build up its audience, although this was not so large as the one that flocked to the Russian seasons. But both the Rambert and Sadlers' Wells companies had faithful followers willing to travel and lead the applause when they went on their short tours. The Sadlers' Wells dancers made their first visit abroad, to Copenhagen, in 1932. But their 1937 season in Paris was of the greatest importance. They were invited by the British Council to represent British Art at the International Exhibition and Ninette de Valois produced her third major ballet for this event. *Checkmate* was tremendously exciting. Sir Arthur Bliss, now Master of the Queen's Musick provided the score and MacKnight Kauffer designed excellent costumes and set,. so that music and design combined to provide Paris with an up-to-date

serious work which is still remarkable even though rarely danced today. It is exciting to remember that when *Checkmate* was first danced English Ballet had made such progress that it received official recognition, while Paris, the first home of classical ballet, was prepared to watch and applaud a company only six years old. Moreover the repertoire was almost entirely created by English choreographers and its dancers had not yet become international stars.

Checkmate was the success of the 1937–38 season. The audience liked its dramatic story of the struggle between Love and Death told through the moves in a game of chess. 'The Red Knight accepts the challenge thrown by the Black Queen at the old Red King. They fight and he wins the struggle. But when he is about to plunge his sword into her heart, he remembers the rose she threw him and hesitates. She seizes his sword and stabs him in the back. Proudly she taunts the old King, then commands her Black Pieces to trap him in their staves. Then the increasing pace and sound of the music builds up the suspense as they entrap the King ever closer. He is trapped. The Black Knights carry their Queen in on high and she steals the Red King's crown before stabbing him to death.'

Checkmate

Sadly enough soon after the London success of *Checkmate*, Dame Lilian Baylis died. She will always be remembered as the one who believed in Ninette de Valois from their first meeting and spared no effort to make the early schemes a reality. Her death put all who worked with her on their mettle, and when the new dressing rooms and ballet studio at the Sadlers' Wells Theatre were completed Ninette de Valois staged *The Sleeping Princess* as a memorial to 'The Lady'. This production had been a long cherished wish, but it was not yet the Beauty it became after the war. Nevertheless on February 2 1939, for the very first time with Robert Helpmann as her Prince, Margot Fonteyn danced Aurora, the rôle that was to make her world-famous ten years later when she appeared in *The Sleeping Beauty* during the Sadlers' Wells Ballet's first visit to New York.

The first English production of *The Sleeping Princess* with Margot Fonteyn, Robert Helpmann and June Brae

That first production of 1939 was officially recognised when the company danced the first two acts at the Gala given in honour of the President of France at Covent Garden in March 1939. When the season ended the company went on tour. Then, after a brief holiday, they visited Manchester, Liverpool and Leeds before returning to London to start the new season, with three performances a week instead of two. But as they travelled home on September 3 1939, war was declared, the theatres were all closed and the company disbanded.

War 1939 – 1945

The closing of the theatres was temporary. Only three weeks later, the expected bombs not having fallen, the Sadlers' Wells Ballet went on tour and, after a brief pause, the Rambert and London ballets started up again. All had to face increasing difficulties. Yet they managed to give even more performances than before to larger audiences all over the British Isles. Nowadays it is difficult to imagine all the problems they had. Now there is no black-out, there are enough dancers and plenty of materials to make costumes, shoes, make-up and scenery. Bombs do not fall on the way to – or in – the theatre. Male dancers are not called-up leaving scarcely enough men to stage a one-act ballet even using young boy students. All these difficulties had to be faced during the war and, worst of all, Ashton and Gore the two leading choreographers, had to go, one into the Air Force, the other to the Navy. But even their departure did not stop new ballets being produced, sometimes in strange places with no stage, like aircraft hangars or workers' canteens. Orchestras disappeared, but with such marvellous musicians as Constant Lambert, Hilda Gaunt and Angus Morrison to play the pianos, there was still music to enjoy. And if things did go wrong – everybody understood and no one left the stage or the theatre

even when bombs fell uncomfortably close. No! we were all in it together and too interested in the ballets because they could make us laugh as well as think; keep us calm or rouse our enthusiasm.

Frederick Ashton

Before Ashton went into the Air Force he created two very different ballets. The first, *Dante Sonata*, in 1940 was a tribute to the Polish people whose country had been over-run in the first days of war. It was staged at the Sadlers' Wells Theatre. Liszt had written the music after reading that part of Dante's great poem *The Divine Comedy* which speaks of souls in purgatory. Working closely with Constant Lambert who orchestrated the music, Ashton told us how 'the Children of Light, trying to break free from their fate, struggle with the Children of Darkness who forever drag them down'. This struggle made us think of the tragedy around us, from which we could see no escape. The choreography was unusual. It was the only time that Ashton ever used barefoot dancers, whose movements expressed freely and profoundly their deepest emotions. The power with which they spoke was so strong that some nights the curtain came down in complete silence, a rare thing in any theatre. It means that the audience has been so caught up in the tragedy that they have forgotten themselves and their surroundings. They feel that the noise of applause would be out of place.

Ashton's *The Wise Virgins* which followed in 1940 was danced to music by Bach in exquisite costumes and set by Rex Whistler. It was the old Bible story, told very simply and calmly, and was a feast for the eyes and ears. It revealed the increasing beauty of Margot Fonteyn's dancing, stressing her hand movements which were inspired by old Italian paintings in which the carefully poised hand suggested words spoken. Even the gaily frivolous Foolish Virgins did not disturb the purity and peacefulness of the pictures made and gave us hope that all would end well.

Dante Sonata

The Quest

Just before he was called up Ashton created *The Wanderer* to the Schubert-Liszt *Fantasie*. It was not successful although the dancing was exciting and included one of the beautiful *pas de deux*, which Ashton creates so marvellously. He so co-ordinates and counter-balances the movements of his two dancers that the lines they make are never strained as they flow together, part and re-join. The patterns made are as important as the steps and poses whether they are strong and clear-cut or softly lyrical. Ashton's other war-time ballet, *The Quest*, with special music by William Walton was also unsuccessful. Based on Spenser's poem *The Faerie Queen*, written in honour of Queen Elizabeth I of England, it is difficult to understand because, like *Ballet Comique de la Reyne*, it is full of allegory. It tells how Saint George of England struggled with and overcame the forces of evil, represented by four knights, to rescue his Lady Una. Such a theme at this time of war should have made us feel proud because it was so patriotic, but perhaps it was too serious when we wanted laughter.

Ninette de Valois

Laughter had certainly been given us by Ninette de Valois after her company had been through a terrifying experience. They had been sent to Belgium and Holland to boost morale at a time when little seemed to be happening on the war front. But they were caught by the German invasion, ultimately escaping in a cargo boat and losing everything belonging to the six ballets they had taken. The war was now on our door-step, so rightly Ninette de Valois decided we wanted laughter to take our minds off such problems, so in 1940 she gave us her riotously funny *The Prospect Before Us*. This was based on a true tale of the London Theatres when Mr. O'Reilly of the Pantheon and Mr. Taylor of the King's Theatre were continually stealing each other's dancers and choreographers, a problem made more

complicated by the burning down of the King's Theatre, the dancers' own rivalries and the demands of the audience for cheaper seats! These 'goings on' can be seen in the cartoons by the artist, Rowlandson, which inspired the choreography as well as the scenery and costumes by Roger Furse. In the ballet we saw the bad-tempered Mons. Noverre and his fussy wife, the jealousy between his two great pupils, Vestris and Didelot and the enchanting Mdlle. Theodore, Didelot's wife. It would be difficult to say which was the funniest moment. But Robert Helpmann as Mr. O'Reilly was largely responsible for them all. His 'hicupping' dance when he had lost dancers, choreographer and theatre to Mr. Taylor and had a final swig at the bottle before taking off the charming solo of Mdlle. Theodore was hilarious. His *ports de bras* were clumsy, his *demi-pointes* weak, his leaps heavy and his *pirouettes* hopeless. Most of us were helpless with laughter, although some thought 'such goings on' had no place in ballet. But they could not deny that such comic episodes have always been part of the English theatre. If Shakespeare and other playwrights can use them, why not our choreographers? The wise ones always do and Ashton and Ninette de Valois paved the way for Cranko and MacMillan after the war.

Robert Helpmann

Robert Helpmann's Mr. O'Reilly was most unexpected, although we should have remembered how funny he had been as the Bridegroom in *The Wedding Bouquet*. He had also danced Albrecht in *Giselle*, Satan in *Job* and acted in the Old Vic production of *A Midsummer Night's Dream* in 1937, where his feeling for the rhythm of the words and his noble movements made him a true Oberon, King of the Fairies. No other dancer had ever played so many different rôles. Unlike many 'stars' he never 'stole the limelight', but lived his part with his colleagues on the stage. This was why he was such a wonderful member of the company. He never tried to do more than he felt he could do well. He was not a virtuoso dancer, but made you believe all difficult steps were easy. If he tried four or five *pirouettes* in class, on stage he would do only two, finishing perfectly on balance. His sympathy with his usual partner, Margot Fonteyn, and with everyone else on stage made the company give of their best.

It was Ashton's call-up and the increasing problem of running both school and company that made Ninette de Valois ask Helpmann to try some choreography. He created five ballets for her before leaving to become an actor and finally Director of the Australian Ballet. Three of his ballets were marvellous pieces of theatre. That is, he used all the resources of the stage, scenery, machinery and lighting to help us understand the tale he unfolded in his choreography. He always placed his dancers in careful relationship to each other, particularly when making their more dramatic gestures. In fact it sometimes seemed as if there was not enough dancing. But learning to act whilst

Ludmila Vlasova and Stanislav Vlasov in the Bolshoi's *The Doves*

Fonteyn and Nureyev in the Royal Ballet's *Romeo and Juliet*

Joseph Scoglio and Marilyn Williams in Ballet Rambert's
Embrace Tiger and Return to Mountain

dancing was important for this company. They were just beginning to understand that every expressive movement made in ballet, as in drama, must be broad, without fuss and carefully timed no matter how slow, fast, dignified or coarse.

Helpmann's first ballet, in 1942, was *Comus* based on the Masque by the great poet, Milton which was performed as a wedding celebration in Ludlow Castle in 1634. It tells how: 'The evil Comus, King of the Underworld, tries to entrap the Innocent Lady, whose Two Brothers attempt her rescue. Comus is too strong for them. But the Lady does not weaken in her resolve to keep away from evil and temptation so Sabrina, the good spirit of the river, overwhelms Comus and his Rout, the Lady and her Brothers are saved'. There were many reasons why we all enjoyed this ballet. Firstly because Purcell's very English music – chosen by Constant Lambert – and Oliver Messel's lovely costumes and set took us back to the time when Comus was first staged. Secondly because Helpmann as Comus spoke some of Milton's words and helped us to understand the true meaning of the story. Like the words of the court-ballets you read about earlier, Milton wrote his words about the Bridgewater family who owned Ludlow Castle and about the river that still flows through its grounds. Lastly there was the way Margot Fonteyn, the Lady, repulsed with simple gestures the evil words spoken by Helpmann as the masterful Comus.

Hamlet Helpmann's next ballet in 1942 was inspired by Shakespeare's description of what happens when a man dies:– 'For in that sleep of death what dreams may come.' As Tchaikovsky's famous music began the curtain went up and we caught our breath as four black-cloaked men bent down and picked up Hamlet's body. As they bore it upstage one arm dropped lifeless and a single light focused on his face. Then, the gloom disappeared and the whole of

Robert Helpmann as Hamlet

Hamlet's tragic life was told, as in the play very quickly, until the moment that he fell dead. The ballet ended as it began. The four black-cloaked men bent down once more and picked up Hamlet's body, but as they carried it up-stage the single light on his face – went out. Everything was over and it seemed such a daring and dramatic ballet. Strangely enough I remember too how Helpmann when acting Hamlet for the Old Vic company seemed to catch his breath, then sat doing nothing, but concentrating on the words spoken by the two grave-diggers. This single movement made us all listen harder.

Although Helpmann's *The Birds* made us laugh because of the antics of a broody Hen in love with a handsome Dove, and a miserable Cuckoo in love with a Nightingale, it was not a success. But soon afterwards in 1944, his *A Miracle in the Gorbals* excited us, though in a very different way. Few choreographers at this time had tried seriously to show life as it can be lived in a real town. The Gorbals was, until very recently, the most sordid part of Glasgow, near the docks and ship-yards, full of smoke, dirt and slums. The ballet showed us that if Christ (called the Stranger) came to earth again, He would again be crucified. The effect this ballet had on my father made me unhappy. He had come from Glasgow and had taught in a Gorbals Sunday school. When the curtain went up and he saw the great black hulk of a ship against the smoky sky and heard the Scottish Lilt and the drone of ships' sirens in the music by Arthur Bliss he sat up straight and tense. When Burra's sordid scene of tenements, pubs, a glimpse of the Clyde and a crowd of rough, dirty Glaswegians come on the stage, he took my hand and whispered: 'It has not changed'. From then on he looked sadly at the tragic story of 'The Stranger who came to save the Young Girl from the river and try to bring some happiness into these grim surroundings. But hate and suspicion turn the crowd against Him. A gang knifed Him to death'. My father covered his face with his hands. He waited a little before we walked out silently. It was a long time before he said: 'I did not believe dancers could make people understand the tragedy of life in the Gorbals. What they have said – is true'. The ballet made a tremendous impression on those of us who believe that Ballet can tell many stories. But this will only be successful when every-one connected with the ballet believes in what is being said and says it simply and clearly through the dancers' movements. *A Miracle in the Gorbals* has been the only ballet in the Sadlers' Wells repertoire in which a choreographer dared to depict a real place and tell a story about people actually seen there. A boy played with an old motor tyre and a tramp looked through the dust-bins. Some people feel that this kind of reality is horrid! For them ballet should only be beautiful and imaginative. But sometimes it must try and show life as it is. After all the old Greek tragedians made their audiences think what would happen if they did wrong. So please allow our choreographers to do the same because they can make us think. Since the war Kenneth MacMillan did just that when he created *The Burrow*, his ballet based on the tragic *Diary of Anne Frank*, a child caught in wartime Holland and taken to be killed in a concentration camp. Another true story to which he gave so much meaning that many sensitive people were made most unhappy and hardly wished to see it again.

War-time Ballet Boom

When the Sadlers' Wells Theatre became a rest centre for people bombed out of their homes, the company made its home in Burnley and began their long war-time tours. They also gave short London seasons at the New (now Albery) Theatre. The Rambert, Arts and London ballets started up at the Arts and Ambassadors Theatres and these ventures became largely successful through the efforts of Peggy Van Praagh. When the 'blitz started no one wanted to be out after dark, so she suggested that ballet should give lunch-time performances like the famous lunch-time concerts started by Dame Myra Hess at the National Gallery. The idea became so successful that if you were in London you could go to the Arts or Ambassadors Theatres, eat lunch and watch ballet between 1 and 2 p.m., Tea ballet between 3.30 and 4.30 p.m. and, when evenings got light, Sherry ballet between 6 and 7 p.m. But the call-up of male dancers and the strain of so many performances made it impossible to carry on. The companies merged under the banner of Marie Rambert and once again her dancers and repertoire were together at the Arts Theatre.

It was in 1939 that Frank Staff's *Peter and the Wolf* became a great favourite. Prokofiev had written his score to help the Moscow Children's audience to understand the sounds made by the various instruments and the way Guy Shepherd, the designer, used things you might pick up if you were playing a game added to the fun. This was the sad tale of a duck swallowed whole by the wolf, despite Peter's efforts to save her. We all know how to make a tree from a step-ladder and two long-handled green mops for the branches and a fine duck pond can be made from a large hoop: You try! It made us all laugh despite the black-out.

Sadly the Arts Theatre was closed by its owner, making it difficult for the Rambert Ballet to carry on until C.E.M.A. (later the Arts Council) began to organise its exhausting war-time tours to hostels, factory canteens and other indescribable corners where they danced to all kinds of audiences. Like the Sadlers' Wells ballet working for E.N.S.A., the other war-time organisation sending out entertainment, particularly to the Forces, they were making friends all the time. This meant that after the war audiences for ballet could be found everywhere, thus helping towns like Manchester and Glasgow to form the Northern Dance Theatre and Scottish Ballet. These and other companies take ballet sometimes to places where no theatres exist. They dance in schools, universities, town-halls and elsewhere in their own areas and give performances equally important to those of the Royal, Festival and visiting companies from all over the world.

Peter and the Wolf. The Duck (Scottish Ballet) and (**above**) the Hunters (Capetown Ballet)

Chapter 5
After the War

Throughout the war the British Isles relied on its own ballets for enjoyment, so imagine the excitement when the Arts Council decided the Sadlers' Wells Ballet should re-open the Opera House, Covent Garden to cheer us up after the bombing was over. On February 23 1946 we put on our best clothes and went to see *The Sleeping Beauty*. I shall never forget the silence when Constant Lambert raised his baton and Tchaikovsky's magical music began, nor the gasp of surprise when the curtains opened and the courtiers began to fill the spacious palace in marvellous costumes designed by Oliver Messel. How had he managed such riches when our clothes were still rationed? But we did not wait for answers for onto the stage stepped a new Margot Fonteyn, a true ballerina, filling it with her beautiful dancing and warm personality. Robert Helpmann too seemed a more noble Prince Charming. He also played the wicked Carabosse as we still had too few male dancers. The rest were in the Forces, or only students who had to be used for the *corps de ballet* and pages.

On that first night a new chapter opened for the company, a chapter in which other countries have a part to play particularly now that so many of our English dancers, teachers and choreographers are in turn playing a part in the development of these new ballet companies everywhere.

The company's performances were so successful that their original engagement of five months was continually extended until they made the Opera House their permanent home. Since 1946 they have presented many new ballets and re-staged old favourites as well as opening in 1947 their school in Baron's Court, where ordinary lessons took their place along with dancing. This was the time when Ninette de Valois was made a Dame of the British Empire for her services to ballet. Shortly after this she formed a new group of dancers to perform with the Sadlers' Wells Opera – now the English National Opera. They were known as the Sadlers' Wells Theatre Ballet, whose aim was to develop the talents of young dancers and choreographers. Amongst them were the late John Cranko, who founded the famous Stuttgart Ballet; Kenneth MacMillan, now director of the Royal Ballet; and Peter Darrell, the director of Scottish Ballet. Their ballets include such favourites as *Pineapple Poll*, *Romeo and Juliet* and *The Tales of Hoffmann*. The company gained its new title of Royal Ballet in 1956 and today uses some one hundred and eighty dancers, the larger group at Covent Garden and the smaller one, known as the New Group, for touring and short seasons sometimes at their old home, the Sadlers' Wells Theatre. The soloists exchange visits. Another six or eight dancers travel with *Ballet For All* under the direction of Alexander Grant, helping audiences everywhere to learn something about ballet. There are now two schools, the one for Seniors at Baron's Court and one for Juniors at White Lodge, Richmond Park, a house originally built for a king's hunting lodge. In addition graduates from the Royal Ballet School's training course for teachers are now taking the English school of classical dance to many countries. Ballets from the repertoire are taken by other companies and taught by dancers and ballet-masters from the Royal Ballet, so English ideas of movement are being spread round the world, just as the Russians spread Diaghilev's ideas after his death.

Schools of Dance

Let us try and understand what is the English School of Classical Dance established by Dame Ninette and Sir Frederick. Whenever I visit older European schools, I am surprised to find that although teachers everywhere use the same rules in class, the dancing always looks different. Perhaps it is the dancers' physique, their temperament, traditional ways of dancing and how it fits to the music. All help to form a national style. The French in Paris were like the courtiers of Louis XIV, elegant and courteous but not very expressive until Serge Lifar gave them greater freedom of movement. My first visit to Milan came when Maestro Cecchetti was still teaching. Under his strict discipline all the dancers were very precise but their bodies were stiff. In Copenhagen the male dancers of the Royal Danish Ballet had the highest, neatest beats I had seen, but the girls were weak despite their lovely elevation and dainty *ports de bras*. But all the Danes excelled in demi-character parts, particularly in their Bournonville ballets which they danced as if they loved them.

Top: Dame Ninette is greeted by all her dancers, pupils and students when she retires

Above: The National Ballet of Canada in *ports de bras*

Right: Ekaterina Maximova of the Bolshoi Ballet

Symphonic Variations

Anne Jenner of the Royal Ballet

A long tour in the Soviet Union brought more surprises. Every school there used the syllabus worked out by Agrippina Vaganova, the great Leningrad teacher. But still the dancing looked different. Because most Soviet stages are large and have a rake (i.e. slope towards the audience) you have to make careful adjustments to your stance and develop a very strong, flexible spine. The dancers' movements are therefore larger and more flowing than elsewhere.

In Leningrad, the second oldest school in the world, the dancers were dignified, graceful without fuss and musically expressive. Vaganova was a pupil of Fokine's and understood his methods of relating dance to music.

In Moscow the dancers excelled in virtuosity. Their elevation and *pirouettes* were 'fabulous'. Much of this knowledge came from Blasis, who taught there for four years, so they still use his valuable rules of balance, *pirouettes* and jumps. 'Bolshoi' means 'big' and this explains why all the dancers at the Bolshoi perform 'big'. But they are not so dignified nor have the beautiful stance of the Georgians in Tbilisi. Few dancers hold their bodies so wonderfully erect or move their arms and heads so freely as the Georgians. Their style comes from their traditional folk dances Yet although their women's *ports de bras* are beautiful, they are not as exquisite as they are in Azerbaijan.

In fact as I went further East the women's *ports de bras* became more important, whilst the men's elevation became more exciting.

Finally there was the American style, first introduced by Ballet Theatre when it visited London in 1946. When the Americans showed us ballets like Jerome Robbins' *Interplay* they seemed more athletic than any before. They were not so elegant and disciplined. But they were full of energy and enjoyed dancing, which is something that too often gets lost when dancers struggle to perfect technique and forget that 'Dance is the thing'.

Sir Frederick's *Symphonic Variations* (1946) is the most beautiful and important example that anyone has yet given of the English style of classical dance. As Dame Ninette said wisely : 'Classical dancing must have order and balance. It needs a calm spaciousness. In its purest form there is no

Above: Laura Connor and **left**: Anthony Dowell of the Royal Ballet

emotion or character. Any expression it has comes through the artistry of any dancer who has mastered its technique'. You may have to read those words several times before you really understand them. Do not worry. *Symphonic Variations* or some other ballet will show you the beautiful patterns classical dance steps and poses can make. Although the music for *Symphonic Variations* was written by a Belgian, César Franck, and its costumes designed by a Russian, Sophie Fedorovitch, it gives you the feeling of an English spring day such as you read about in poems by Shakespeare, Shelley and Keats. The six dancers have come together in the cool of the morning to enjoy their relationships with each other as they weave their way through the music and flowing patterns Sir Frederick has made. Nothing disturbs their feelings for the dance. Neither one nor the other dominates the stage. Like English country

79

Ronald Emblem as Mother Simone in *La Fille Mal Gardée*

dancers they meet as equals and show us that the English style is spacious, disciplined and well-balanced like the patterns of those old dances. It uses longer phrases of movement which do not always repeat as they do in Petipa's choregraphy. Each part of an *enchainement* covers more of the stage and allows each dancer greater freedom. But this also means that he or she must be more disciplined than usual because each one is only part of the whole pattern and must not spoil the lines and shapes being drawn. Because each dancer is equally important no one must show off.

However English dancers can show off if the ballet requires them to do so, like Antoinette Sibley, Merle Park, Anthony Dowell and Michael Coleman among others with their brilliant swift foot-work, elevation and *pirouettes*. Others show off in a different way, like Alexander Grant dancing *sur les pointes* as Bottom, or Ronald Emblem doing his clog dance as Mother Simon or David Wall as an actor-dancer in many rôles. Remember that Sir Frederick made their dances as well as many others since he joined Dame Ninette to make ballets in 1935. He continued to make them when he became Director of the Royal Ballet on her retirement, and still does so occasionally even now he too has retired. Kenneth MacMillan, now Director of the Royal Ballet has followed his example and shows that he too has mastered the English lyrical style in his beautiful *pas de deux*, such as that of *Concerto* and the charming dances he created for Juliet's friends in his *Romeo and Juliet*. He has learnt Dame Ninette's lesson that: 'The arms are the framework to the head and body. They play a vital part in conveying expression and meaning. Without sensitive hands and arms, the dancer is dumb'.

World Touring Companies

1. French Ballet

When Serge Lifar became Professor of Dance as well as chief soloist and choreographer of the Paris Opera in 1932 he was determined to restore French ballet to the foremost place it had occupied at the time of Louis XIV. He began to stage stories of great gods and heroes as done before the 1789 Revolution. But first he had to train more male dancers because they were so few. The ballets in the repertoire were also very old-fashioned and it took him some time to create new ones. Some of these, like *Alexander the Great* in 1937 were grand spectacles. Others were more like the experiments Diaghilev had made during the last six years of his life. Lifar believed that he alone could create all things needed for a ballet and often arranged dances before ordering the sounds, rhythms and phrases he needed from a composer. His first experiment was the old story of *Icarus*, which proved that you could dance without music, as some Yugoslav and other folk dancers do. Such dancers' feet and clapping hands do create exciting sounds. But classical dance is silent. Lifar's experiment did not work. We spend much time learning how to land softly from a jump and no one would believe in Wilis and Fairies if their *pointe* shoes clattered on the wooden boards. So if a ballet has no music, and is danced classically, it lacks the drive and rhythm music can give it. But the Opera Ballet did not visit London before 1954 by which time we had already enjoyed *Les Ballets des Champs Elysées*.

Roland Petit's *Ballets des Champs Elysées* were our first French visitors to London after the War and showed us nothing like the grand-opera ballet *Les Indes Galants* by Rameau which the opera brought over later. Although Petit had been a student of Lifar, his ideas were very different. Like Robert Helpmann he realised that everyday events could inspire a ballet. I remember the lively *Le Bal des Blanchisseuses*, where washerwomen gaily danced among their laundry and one young girl showed off her

Lesley Collier as Juliet

acrobatic tricks. Another, *Les Forains* showed a travelling circus arriving at the ground, putting up their tent and giving their show, before departing sadly because the audience rewarded them so little. It gave us two sides of the 'travellers'' life. Once the show is on, all is glamour, excitement and magic, because you are on show in the ring. But when the tent is folded, there is only hard work, little money, perhaps despair. But there is comradeship.

Petit always made fascinating use of every-day movement and behaviour so that his characters came to life on the stage. His most dramatic attempt was in *Le Jeune Homme et la Mort* in 1946. This told the tragedy of a young man who hangs himself because his girl friend tells him to go. The way she kicked him to the floor in his sordid garret before stalking off, was horrible. Petit used the same type of movement when he turned the opera *Carmen* into a ballet. These movements are based on what you and I do when we lose our tempers. They had never been so used until Robert Helpmann and Petit showed us how they could become part of dance. But you cannot keep to cool and dignified classical rules when you make them.

Labyrinth with Deanne Bergsma

Field Figures with Rudolph Nureyev and Monica Mason

Left: Peter Darrell's *Scorpius* using movements like those of Roland Petit

Petit also became very interested in the use of elaborate machinery, lighting, film strips and other effects, particularly when he based his ballets on plays and novels that needed quick changes of scene. These ideas often hindered the dancing but demonstrated how all kinds of things, the 'Multi-media', as they are called, can be used to create what is called 'total theatre'.

'Total theatre' is often the kind of entertainment produced by Maurice Béjart, whose Twentieth Century Ballet has its home in Brussels, and by many American leaders of Modern Dance groups like Alwin Nikolais. Such entertainments occupy little space in this history. Nevertheless Béjart's dancers mostly have a sound classical training and adapt themselves to many different styles as do any company having only a few modern dance ballets in their repertoire. After all Glen Tetley's *Field Figures* and Hans Von Manen's *Grosse Fuge* and *Twilight* are danced by the Royal and other companies. Other choreographers everywhere create ballets using similar modern dance techniques. These were all influenced by the Central European School of Dancing led by Mary Wigman and Rudolph Von Laban, whose pioneer work inspired Kurt Jooss, a name which must never be forgotten, because he made modern dance acceptable to large audiences.

Agon with Laura Connor

Kurt Jooss and The Green Table 1933

The Central European School of Dancing grew after the 1914–18 War. It aimed to examine how and why we all made movement. Kurt Jooss came from this school and used the movements analysed to express the moods, emotions and actions of the characters in his ballets. His most important one was *The Green Table*. It tried to tell you what happens if nations sign an unfair Peace Treaty. 'The curtain goes up. The diplomats are sitting and arguing at a large green table. Suddenly one of them becomes furious and fires his pistol. Then follow scenes of men marching away

to war, mothers, wives and children weeping, old men and other women working in factories, the men fighting and dying. Through each scene stalks the figure of Death until no more young men are left. Again the diplomats sit and argue at the green table. Again the pistol is fired'. We were already worried by what was happening in Europe when we first saw this ballet. It made us think, like Igor Belsky's *Leningrad Symphony* commemorating the terrible siege of Leningrad during the 1939–45 War. Both ballets helped us to understand how better to try and arrange things, even the movements of our dancers.

The ideas of the Central European School are still being used widely throughout America and Europe, so when modern ballets are danced side by side with old favourites, it is made easier to understand the differences between the free movements of the modern style and the discipline of the classical ballets. However some modern choreographers only work with their own group. Their work can be very difficult to understand without a lot of reading or research. But that is not what a ballet should be like. Fokine once told me that if I had to read the story on my programme then the dancers were not doing their jobs properly!

2. The American Ballets

Ballet Theatre from America were our second visitors in 1946 and showed us that they too were borrowing stories from real life. Their *Fancy Free* was 'just our cup of tea'. The choreographer, Jerome Robbins showed us 'three sailors on leave calling at a bar for a drink. Here they picked up three girls and told them how bravely they had behaved in battle. One jumped on to the counter and showed his girl how he had brought down an enemy plane single-handed. Another kept his eye on his girl as he danced in slow motion. The third was a little crazy and showed off. But the girls got bored and left. The three sailors had to start all over again!' We had seen it all before in our ports during the war. Certainly the uniforms were different, as was the dancing because we had not seen much jitterbug, jive and the rest at that time. But the jokes were the same as ours and we laughed at them. Just as we laughed at Agnes de Mille's *Rodeo*. In this the plainest and clumsiest girl on the ranch, a tom-boy, finally wins the handsomest cowboy at the barn dance. The music by Aaron Copland was fascinating but the most exciting part of the ballet had no music at all. After the ranch hands had rounded up the cattle and gone to prepare for the barn dance, the stage grew dark. Then we heard the sounds of dancing feet and handclapping. As it grew lighter there were all the cow-girls and boys doing a 'running set', a typical folk dance. The sounds they made, made us want to join in, so all of us, from the amphitheatre to the stalls, began to clap in rhythm and thus became part of the fun.

Although Jerome Robbins and Agnes de Mille were not the first to show American life in ballet, Ballet Theatre were the first to show London that not only could Americans create their own ballets. They also had their own school of classical dance. This had been started when Lincoln Kerstein persuaded Balanchine to develop a school and company in New York, from which he would be able to prove that Americans too had something fresh to give to ballet. Since 1934 Balanchine has formed that school, often

Above and below: the Nederlands Dans Theater in ballets by Hans van Manen

The Lesson by Flemming Flindt

guided by the wisdom of Lincoln Kerstein. There have been many ups and downs and many changes in personnel. Balanchine has also created many ballets for this, now foremost, American company, The New York City Ballet. Many of its ballets are without a story and show how straightforward and energetic these dancers are. Stravinsky has composed many scores for Balanchine, some of which like *Agon* and *Orpheus* are danced by other companies. But Balanchine has never produced a really successful American ballet. This has been done by Americans. The first was *Billy the Kid* in 1939 and told the story of a well-known American outlaw. The choreographer, Eugene Loring used the antics and ways of cowboys and Indians as well as the practices of pioneers and trusty sheriffs travelling over wide open spaces, to inspire his dances. His cast played cards, drank, galloped, shot, in fact did all the things you see in any Western film. See if you can crack a whip, ride a bucking horse or throw a lassoo as you dance. This will give you some idea of what movements were used in *Billy the Kid* and *Rodeo*.

Agnes de Mille's masterpiece was *Fall River Legend* in 1948. This told the true tale of Lizzie Borden:– 'Whose mother died. Her father married again and the step-mother was jealous and suspicious of everything Lizzie did. The poor girl became so distraught that in a frenzy of anger, she took an axe and killed her father and step-mother. She was

hanged.' It was a grim ballet. You could compare it with *Giselle* because both heroines go mad. But Giselle loses her reason because Albrecht forsakes her, Lizzie because she feels she is hated. Thus the two characters are very different. With every dramatic ballet seen, you gain better understanding of why dancers' movements are always changing. Although the human body has not changed for thousands of years, choreographers are always finding new ways of using human movements. They have to work out all the details for each character in a story and make each character fit in with the others and the plot. This is difficult if the plot deals with real life. We do not dance our way through life, but choreographers have to make us believe we do in ballets like *A Miracle in the Gorbals, Le Bal des Blanchisseuses, Fancy Free* and *Fall River Legend*.

3. The Royal Danish Ballet

Our third important visitors to London were the Royal Danish Ballet, who came in 1953. One of the happiest jobs I had to do as a critic was to go to Copenhagen with some fellow critics and help these delightful dancers decide if they were good enough to show themselves outside Denmark. We were royally entertained and the ten day visit went all too quickly. I spent much time watching classes and rehearsals taken by the ballet-master, Harald Lander and the famous old dancer, Hans Brenaa, whose special knowledge of Bournonville's class work made me understand what difficulties of style had to be mastered before appearing in ballets like *La Sylphide* and *Napoli*. Needless to say we all fell in love with Denmark and the dancers because of their whole-hearted love and performances of Bournonville's unique ballets. The mixture between their old and new repertoire could not have been more marked. One of the new ones, *Qaartsiluni* was Harald Lander's attempt to show us an ancient Eskimo ritual. 'When the first rays of sun begin to rise over the horizon after the long dark winter, an old Eskimo priest calls on his tribe to worship the dawn.' The throb of the music, the increasing speed and passion of the dancers made me realise how important the sun was to these people, just as the earth had been to the Russian tribes in *The Rite of Spring*. In complete contrast to this strangely moving ballet was Lander's *Études*, now a favourite ballet for several companies. In it Lander wished to show all the exercises performed by the Royal Danish dancers from the moment they enter the school to the time when they retire, and from the first *pliés* to the final great leaps and *pirouettes* round the stage, introduced by him after studying Russian methods. He realised that time can never stand still if ballet is to progress. *Études* was a modern version of Bournonville's *Konservatoriet*. To see both ballets is to realise how dancing has changed.

Flemming Flindt, Lander's pupil is now director and choreographer for the Royal Danish Ballet. He believes in preserving the old and bringing in the new. He borrows ballets from other countries when he feels it necessary, but adds new ones of his own. These can be fascinating because he is interested in modern plays and sometimes uses their plots to inspire his works. Some are gay and simple, some highly dramatic, like *The Dancing Lesson*, a tragedy of a teacher driving a pupil too hard. He also uses the 'multi-

Maya Plissetskaya and Maris Liepa in *Anna Karenina*

Maris Liepa as Crassus

media' like Béjart. But because his dancers are such wonderful actors, everything they perform makes the meaning of his stories very clear.

4. The Bolshoi and Kirov Ballets

Only those of us who had visited Russia after the Revolution knew that their great traditions of dance had been maintained and strengthened by the work of that wonderful teacher, Agrippina Vaganova. We knew that when the Bolshoi first visited London in 1956 there would be wonderful dancing in the old favourites. But what would

audiences think of their *Romeo and Juliet* and their star, Galina Ulanova? We need not have worried. On their first night her exquisite dancing as Juliet and her later performances as Giselle captured everyone's imagination. In fact it was the magnificent dancing of the whole company that excited us for they lived every moment of their lives on the stage.

Few Soviet ballets have shown us much new by way of choreography. But they always impress us by their storytelling particularly in *Romeo and Juliet*. The music was composed by Prokofiev working with a Shakespearean expert. They wanted to tell the story of these 'star-crossed lovers' as in the play. But when the score was finished, it was rejected as being too modern and undanceable – like Tchaikovsky's score for *Swan-Lake* had been originally. However in 1939 Leonide Lavrovsky, the Leningrad choreographer, successfully interpreted Prokofiev's music and translated Shakespeare's words into dance. Beautiful *pas de deux* replaced the poetry. Instead of angry, dramatic speeches there were fights and deaths. Comic dances replaced the joking. Kenneth MacMillan produced a version of *Romeo and Juliet* for The Royal Ballet, Sir Frederick made one for the Royal Danish company and there are other versions. In all of them you will hear how Prokofiev painted the characters and scenes in the life of Verona, constantly being interrupted by the quarrels

The Capetown University Ballet, **top:** David Poole's *Rain Queen* and
above: Gary Burne's *Variations within Space*

between Montagues and Capulets. No sooner have you
seen the first fights and deaths than the curtain re-opens on
Juliet playing with her dolls. Her nurse tells her she is
growing up and her parents introduce her to Paris, the
kinsman they wish her to marry. But Romeo comes to the
ball celebrating the betrothal and he and Juliet fall in love.
And so the story of the 'star-crossed lovers' unfolds until
they lie dead in their tomb. We still weep at their tragedy.

Since 1956 the Bolshoi, Kirov and other Soviet dancers
have visited the West yet few of their ballets have had the
same success as *Romeo and Juliet*, although the magnificent
dancing of their stars has never been questioned. The
brilliant technique of Maya Plissetskaya, Nina Timofeyeva,

Ekaterina Maximova, Irina Kolpakova, Nina Sorokina,
Natalie Bessmertnova with such partners as Fadeyechev,
Vassilyev, Lavrovsky, Soloviev, Vladimirov and many
others is matched by their ability to act out their rôles. It
is this quality which made such an impression in *Spartacus*
with choreography by Grigorovitch to music by Khat-
chaturian. The story is based on a true tale of the Roman
Empire when the slaves revolted against the tyrant, Crassus.
The barbaric dancing of the Roman warriors led by Crassus
made us all understand why Diaghilev's *Polovtsian
Warriors* took everyone's breath away when they first
appeared in Paris in 1909. I still find it very difficult to
believe that Maris Liepa playing the evil tyrant can be the

same dancer who dances the heart-broken Albrecht in *Giselle*. And he is not the only Soviet star capable of so changing his personality on the stage that one scarcely recognises the courteous teacher greeting you before taking a class at the school.

Many Soviet ballets have serious themes dealing with the times in which we live. But their audiences can also laugh as they did in *Lieutenant Kije*. This was also based on a true story – or so they say! 'When making a list of officers to be promoted, a clerk made an ink blot. A higher official not daring to admit he could not read, called out "Lieutenant Kije". So Tsar Paul promoted the imaginary officer by stages to the highest rank. Then, because he could rise no higher, gave him a magnificent funeral during which the dancer, representing the "Blot" whirled across the stage for the last time'.

There are now over thirty ballet companies producing old favourites as well as ballets inspired by the folk tales of their own republics, by famous novels like *Anna Karenina*, by poems or current events. There are some which display the particular qualities of the dancers. In addition most Soviet Republics have their own folk dance groups. The most important of these have travelled widely to show the rich dance traditions of Georgia, the Ukraine, or, like the Moiseyev State Ensemble, a tremendous variety of ideas ranging from an exquisite ancient Georgian ritual to a riotous present-day Football Match. Such riches can be compared with those of other visitors from China, Latin America, Africa, India, Poland, Hungary, Spain – but why go on? Every country has its rich heritage of dance and today's audience's learn from such visitors. Few of them stage what we could call a ballet. But they do tell us about their traditional ways. Some of these are very like our own and very often some tradition or another inspires a choreographer.

Visitors from Overseas

Perhaps the most important visitors to London after the war were those students who came to study and rose to become stars of the Royal Ballet – for example Nadia Nerina and Merle Park – or, more excitingly, returned to their own countries or went on to other parts of the world. There they have contributed much, and like the late John Cranko, started new schools and companies often with colleagues from England. The influence of these dancers, teachers and choreographers is so widespread that I would have to write another book to tell you all about them. Here I can only mention a few because ballet owes them so much.

The three names mentioned above came from South Africa or Rhodesia, and with David Poole, Alfred Rodrigues, Patricia Miller and others played and still play an important part in the success of the Sadlers' Wells and Royal Ballet. David Poole is now in charge of the Capetown University Ballet and its school. Alfred Rodrigues spends much time travelling to produce old and his own new works in places as far apart as Turkey and Japan. The late John

Top and above: John Cranko's *The Taming of the Shrew* with Marcia Haidée and Richard Cragun

Cranko's Stuttgart Ballet is tremendously important. He founded both company and school and created an unique repertoire. His *The Taming of the Shrew* is a brilliant interpretation of Shakespeare's play and his *Eugene Onegin* translates Tchaikovsky's opera into dance. All his ballets contain wonderful *pas de deux*, particularly in *The Taming of the Shrew*. These are amazing mixtures of angry quarrels,

The Australian Ballet in Robert Helpmann's *Sun Music*

downright fisticuffs and tender caresses, just as Shakespeare described the battle of wits between Katherine and Petruchio. John Cranko has left a rich legacy of ballet to the town where Noverre was first allowed to produce ballets in which dancers acted out worthwhile plots. Cranko's colleagues will surely cherish his work as well as dancing in the very different modern-style ballets produced by their new director, the American Glen Tetley. They have the discipline, technique and insight into expressive movement that John Cranko gave them.

Gwyneth Lloyd first started a school and company in Canada in 1938. This became known as the Royal Winnipeg Ballet in 1951 when it danced before Queen Elizabeth II. Canada has several other exciting companies, too, the most

important now being the National Ballet of Canada. On the advice of Dame Ninette, Betty Oliphant laid the foundation of a National School in Toronto in 1951 and, with Celia Franca as artistic director, developed this into the successful company which boasts an impressive list of stars and ballets, and whose tours abroad, especially in the U.S.S.R. have interested large audiences.

Dame Peggy Van Praagh has done so much to encourage young dancers and choreographers since giving up her own dancing career in 1946 to become ballet-mistress, later assistant director of the Sadlers' Wells Theatre Ballet, that it is difficult to know what has been the most important part of her work. Since leaving the company in 1956, she has produced old favourites as well as ballets by Dame Ninette,

A modern work from the Canadian National Ballet

Sir Frederick and Anthony Tudor for many European countries as well as teaching in America and elsewhere. But in 1960 she began what must be considered her greatest effort for which she was honoured with the title of Dame. In 1959 she went to Australia to become Artistic Director of the Borovansky Ballet, whose founder had just died. From this group of dancers she gradually built what is now the Australian Ballet. She established its own school in 1964 and a year later was joined as co-director by Sir Robert Helpmann. Since then the company has grown in strength and fame. Sir Robert has produced some interesting ballets like *Sun Music* based on Australian and other themes as well as directing a film of the ballet, *Don Quixote*, starring himself, Rudolph Nureyev and Lucette Aldous.

New Zealand too has made its contribution to the stars of the Royal Ballet. Alexander Grant was one of the first to arrive in 1946 and immediately attracted attention with his ability to act and dance a part. Sir Frederick has made many rôles to display these unique gifts. No one has yet matched Grant's performances as Alain in *La Fille Mal Gardée* or Bottom in *The Dream*. He can make us laugh as well as bring tears to our eyes with the tragedies of these simple folk who never get the girl of their dreams, Lisa or The Fairy Queen. Sara Neil and Rowena Jackson were other New Zealanders to become stars for the Royal Ballet. The latter eventually returned home with her husband, Phillip Chatfield to re-form a company, originally started by a Danish dancer, and a school which may well become as famous as those run by their old colleagues elsewhere in the Commonwealth.

But these are not the only members of The Royal Ballet to develop schools and companies. Dame Ninette herself started the ballet school in Turkey to provide dancers and create ballets for the Opera House being built in Ankara. She has advised many other schools and companies on teaching methods, choregraphy and the hundred and one things she has done for her own company. Mary Skeaping, who acted as ballet-mistress to the Sadlers' Wells and other companies, finally became ballet-mistress and principal teacher for the Royal Swedish Ballet and its school. John Field, who had directed the Royal Ballet touring company helping to develop the talents of stars like Doreen Wells and David Wall, then became director of the ballet at La Scala, Milan, the home of Blasis. He is now Artistic Director of the R.A.D.

Finale

Thus in 1976 we find a love of ballet has grown throughout the world and many people from many countries have made their contribution to its changes and successes since the first *ballets de cour* of the sixteenth century. You may think I have not mentioned some of your favourite ballets or dancers. Perhaps you think I have mentioned too many you have not seen. But I have tried to write about those which brought something new to their audiences. I wanted to help you understand what makes some ballets live, and who created them. Here are some of the reasons.

1. Some ballets live because they appeal to all ages and all kinds of people and because the characters are a little like ourselves, as they are in *La Fille Mal Gardée*.

2. Some live because they have, among other things, a wonderful score written by great composers like Tchaikovsky and Stravinsky.

3. Some live because they make us laugh like *Fancy Free*, *Rodeo*, *Pineapple Poll* and *The Taming of the Shrew*.

4. Some live because they have a fantastic story like *The Firebird* and *Ondine*.

5. Some live because they make you think, like *The Green Table*, *The Rake's Progress*, *Job* and *The Miracle in the Gorbals*.

6. Some live because they unfold great dramas like *Petrushka*, *Romeo and Juliet* and *Fall River Legend*.

7. Some live because of their romantic story like *La Sylphide* and *Giselle*.

8. Some live because they are danced for the sheer fun of it like *Façade* and *Les Patineurs*.

9. Some live because they show us the beauty of the dancers' movements like Sir Frederick's *Symphonic Variations*, Balanchine's *Serenade*, Kenneth MacMillan's *Concerto* and Jerome Robbins' *The Afternoon of a Faun*.

10. And some live because they try to show us the doings of us, quite ordinary people. Sir Frederick has even dared to give the real names of the characters in *Enigma Variations*. Elgar dedicated his music to 'My friends pictured within', and Sir Frederick has tried to show them as they really were.

Top: *Concerto* by Kenneth MacMillan with Alfreda Thorogood and Donald MacLeary

Above: Anthony Dowell and Antoinette Sibley in Kenneth MacMillan's *Manon*

Enigma Variations. **Left:** Svetlana Beriosova and Derek Rencher as Mrs and Mr Elgar

Below: Wayne Sleep as Doctor Sinclair, whose dog fell in the river

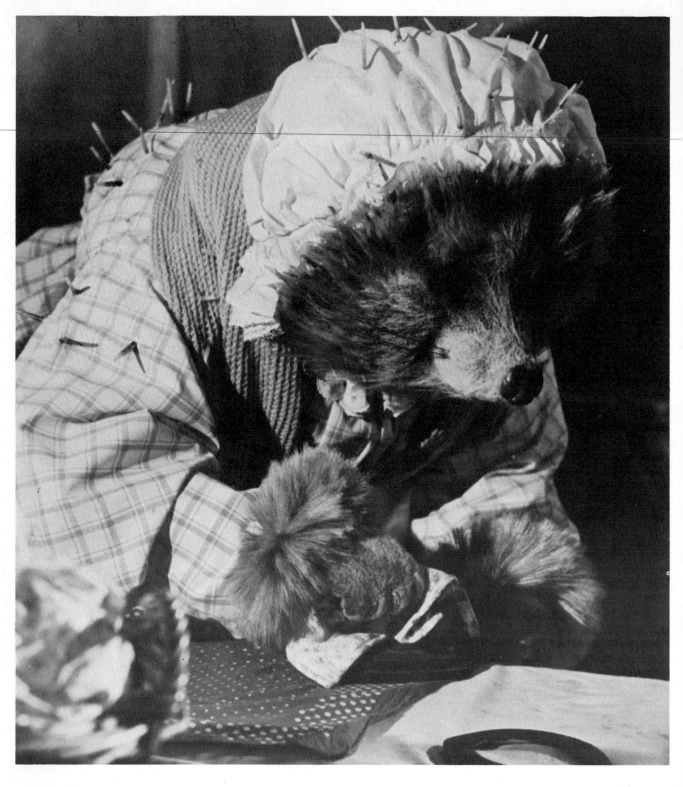

Sir Frederick Ashton as Mrs Tiggy-winkle from *The Tales of Beatrix Potter*

As a little girl I had met one of these people. When he walked on stage I could not believe my eyes as he placed his hand on Elgar's shoulder. For I remembered how he had placed his hand on mine in the very same way when he was told, I was going to be a dancer. He then said as he looked hard at me: 'You will'. I believed him.

To create such true expression in dance is the stroke of a genius. It is only one of the many strokes of genius that the dancers, teachers and choregraphers have made ever since the beginnings of ballet and which they will continue to make as long as people love the dance – and that means as long as there are people!

Index

95